ILLUSTRATED LIBRARY OF COOKING

VOLUME 15 Sod-Ste

Like sodas? And sundaes and
shakes and splits and all the
Soda Fountain Sensations? Go
for sizzling steaks and chops
grilled indoors or out? Or a
robust, tomatoey budget-style
steak? You'll find an entire
mini-book devoted to luscious
ice cream concoctions, another
to steaks and chops. And
that's not all! There's one
more mini-book: Soup Kettle.

ROCKVILLE HOUSE PUBLISHERS, INC.
ROCKVILLE CENTRE, NEW YORK 11570

VOLUME 15

Family Circle®

Illustrated Library of

COOKING

YOUR READY REFERENCE FOR A LIFETIME OF GOOD EATING

Picture Credits:

California Beef Council ● Chiquita Brands, Inc. ● Diet Delight ● National Live Stock and Meat Board ● George Nordhausen

Regal Rio Sundae

Table of Contents

SODA FOUNTAIN

SENSATIONS

SODA FOUNTAIN SENSATIONS AND OTHER FANTASTIC FROZEN DESSERTS: TIPS ON BUYING ICE CREAMS, HOMEMADE ICE CREAMS, SHERBETS AND ICES, SUNDAES, SPLITS AND ALASKAS, SAUCES FOR ICE CREAM DESSERTS, SODAS, SHAKES AND FROSTS

Although we think of ice creams and the whole repertoire of frozen desserts as American, most of them are not. Frozen ices were popular in Italy as long ago as the 16th century. Chefs of Catherine de Médicis introduced them to France at the time she married Henry II, creating during the prolonged wedding festivities a new flavor every day.

The French court was mad for the Italian ices and later so was the rest of France. It was while in France that Thomas Jefferson sampled a particularly good ice cream and copied down the recipe in his own hand. He served ice cream at the White House as did George Washington before him and Dolley Madison after him.

Chocolate lovers can never get enough chocolate, so for them what better than satin-cool Chocolate Ice Cream Supreme made with both cocoa and sweet cooking chocolate? To top, a chocolate sauce, extra dark and rich.

The ice-cream cone and soda are American, however. Both were created quite by accident, both at expositions. The cone came about when an ice-cream merchant at the St. Louis World's Fair in 1904 ran out of dishes in which to serve ice cream. He dashed to a baker across the way and bought thin cookies that could be rolled into cones. The soda was invented some 30 years earlier in Philadelphia at the semicentennial of the Franklin Institute. There was a record-breaking hot spell, and the ice-cream merchant sat sadly watching his ice creams melt into slush until, in a moment of ingenuity, he mixed the soft ice cream with seltzer water and produced the first ice-cream soda. It was the hit of the semicentennial.

In the following pages you will find a good selection of soda recipes, also recipes for dozens of other soda fountain sensations, recipes for ice creams you can make in both freezer and refrigerator and directions for turning commercial ice creams into a variety of festive frozen desserts.

1799

Mint ice cream, pear halves and chocolate shavings.

TIPS ON BUYING ICE CREAMS, SHERBETS AND ICES

1800

Americans eat more than a billion gallons of ice cream a year. And that doesn't include sherbet, ice milk, water ice or any of a dozen other frozen desserts, each of which has its own personality. How much do you know about what you're getting every time you reach into your supermarket's freezer cabinet?

THE CHOICES:

Ice Cream—Way out front in popularity, this smoothie owes its creamy goodness to a just-right blend of milk, cream, sweetening and flavoring. The kinds of milk and cream that go into it depend upon the manufacturer's own recipe, and each adds fruits, nuts, candy, chocolate, cocoa, coffee or other ingredients to create the dozens of exciting flavors we know today. PREMIUM marked on the carton means that the ice cream contains extra milk fat and higher quality other ingredients, and usually it has less air whipped into it during freezing, making it richer.

French Ice Cream or French Custard Ice Cream—Either of these names tells you that the product contains more eggs or egg yolks than other frozen desserts. Most homemade ice creams fall into this category.

Diabetic or Dietetic Ice Cream—Many supermarkets now stock an ice-cream product labeled in either of these two ways. Exact recipes vary from state to state, and are regulated by the states, but all diabetic ice creams are artificially sweetened.

Mellorine—Available in only a few areas, this treat looks and tastes like ice cream but is made with vegetable or animal fat as a substitute for milk fat.

Ice Milk—This frosty is rapidly becoming a regular in many homes. Compared to ice cream, ice milk contains fewer milk solids but usually more sugar. Many weight-watchers think ice milk ranks considerably lower than ice cream in calories. Here's how the counts stack up: ½ cup vanilla ice milk equals 114 calories, the same amount of vanilla ice cream is 132 calories.

Soft-Frozen Dairy Desserts—Popularly called frozen custard, it is creamy-soft, smooth and ready for eating just as it comes from the freezing machine.

Sherbet—After a big meal, on a sizzling day or any time at all, this tart cooler tastes so refreshing. Recipes combine dairy ingredients, sweeting, fruit or juice and fruit acid.

Ice—Some folks think of sherbet and ice as the same, but they do differ. Ice is considered a non-dairy food, as it's made of water, sugar and fruit or juice, but no milk products. Sometimes called "Italian water ice."

Spumoni—This Italian treat sometimes comes packed as serving-size wedges, individually wrapped, or it may boast a large bowl shape with an outer layer of vanilla ice cream and a center of chocolate, fruit or macaroon mousse.

Tortoni—Here's another familiar Italian specialty that starts with regular ice cream. Extra cream is added, then the mixture is frozen in individual molds and topped with macaroon crumbs.

Other Prizes—Depending on where you live, you'll find many selections. To name just a few: Ice-cream cakes made of one or more layers of ice cream and a sweetened whipped-cream frosting; ice-cream pies with a single layer of ice cream handsomely frosted and decorated; frozen puddings of ice cream or egg-rich custard and fruits, nuts or flavorings; and frozen bars, sticks, sandwiches or cones. Almost all are ice cream, ice milk or sherbet, and usually bars and sticks are coated with chocolate, candy, nuts or other goodies.

Getting More for Your Money:

Most ice creams, ice milks or sherbets come in handy pint, half-gallon and gallon containers, and you'll even find tiny cups holding a single serving. Many families say it's hard to buy too much, and if you have the freezer space, be thrifty and choose the largest cartons. Watch, too, for your supermarket's advertised specials on the most popular flavors, another key to economical shopping. And by saving on the dependables, you can splurge once in a while on a specialty item to pamper your family or dress up a meal. Premium ice cream, of course, carries a price tag to match its deluxe quality. Knowing how appetites for ice cream differ, it's difficult to suggest a serving guide, but here's a starter: Figure 3 or 4 servings from a pint, 5 or 6 servings if your dessert is à la mode.

Tips on Storing Ice Creams

Like all dairy foods, frozen desserts are perishable and must be taken care of properly if you are to enjoy them at their best. Holding them at a low temperature (below zero) and keeping them tightly wrapped are the most important musts. Other reminders:

Keep ice creams from ups and downs in temperature, and this means to return the carton to the freezer before the ice cream melts. Partial melting and refreezing cause it to become icy or coarse.

After removing part of the ice cream from its container, press a small piece of foil, wax paper or transparent wrap against the surface of what's left to keep out the air and prevent a waxlike film from forming on top. Reseal the carton and return it to the freezer.

If you buy in quantity, date all cartons before storing, then keep tabs on the dates.

Plan to store ice cream in your freezer no longer than two months and in the freezer compartment of a refrigerator for two to three weeks.

Some Serving Tricks with Ice Creams

When it comes to serving, temperature is as important as it is for storing, and ice cream

1801

An old-time, all-time American classic: a lattice top sweet red cherry pie topped with a scoop of ice cream.

tastes best slightly softened. Remove the carton from the freezer and let stand at room temperature about 10 minutes or in the refrigerator for a half hour. Always a delight plain, it's even better in one of these dressy, but easy, treats:

Make a fancy baked Alaska this simple way: Spoon 2 pints of ice cream into a mixing bowl and freeze until very firm. Place a packaged plain cake layer on a cookie sheet; unmold ice cream on top, then trim the layer to within ½ inch of ice cream. Frost all over with meringue, spreading it carefully to cover cake and ice cream completely. Slide into hot oven (425°) for 5 minutes, or just until meringue is tipped with gold. Remove to a chilled plate and serve immediately.

Buy a ready-prepared graham-cracker or chocolate pie shell, or make your own, and fill with scoops of ice cream. Drizzle with a bottled sundae sauce of your choice, chocolate or maple-flavor syrup or melted jelly. Or sprinkle with lightly salted chopped nuts.

Toast thin slices of pound cake. Put each two together, sandwich style, with a square of ice cream and top with whipped cream.

Swirl crunchy peanut butter through slightly softened vanilla or chocolate ice cream. Equally delicious is canned pie filling stirred in as the flavor dividend.

Frost a half-gallon brick of your favorite ice cream with sweetened whipped cream or a whipped topping. Decorate with cut-up maraschino cherries or with jumbo walnut or pecan halves and freeze until serving time.

Slice ice cream into serving-size squares and coat with flaked coconut. Spoon thawed frozen orange-juice concentrate over each.

Stir vanilla ice cream to soften, spoon on top of a pan of brownies and freeze. When ready to serve, cut into squares and drizzle with mint syrup.

1802

SOME HOMEMADE ICE CREAMS, SHERBETS AND ICES

Old-Fashioned Vanilla Ice Cream
Makes about 2½ quarts

6 egg yolks
1⅓ cups sugar
½ teaspoon salt
4 cups milk, scalded
2 cups cream for whipping
2 tablespoons vanilla

1 Beat egg yolks with sugar and salt in a medium-size saucepan; stir in 2 cups of the milk. Heat slowly, stirring constantly, *just* until sugar dissolves. Pour into a large bowl; chill until mixture is cold.
2 Stir in remaining milk, cream and vanilla. Pour into 16-cup can of an electric or hand-crank ice cream freezer. Freeze, following manufacturer's directions.
3 Unsnap cranking gear; carefully wipe cover and around side of can with a damp cloth. Lift off lid; remove dasher. Serve immediately. Or, to hard-freeze, repack following manufacturer's directions; let stand two hours. To store in your freezer, lift can from pail and wipe outside to remove all ice and salt; cover. Place in freezer until serving time.

Milk-Chocolate Ice Cream
Makes about 3 quarts

3 eggs
½ cup sugar
¼ teaspoon salt
7 cups cream for whipping
2 jars (10 ounces each) fudge topping for ice cream
1 tablespoon vanilla

1 Beat eggs with sugar and salt in a medium-size saucepan; stir in 2 cups of the cream. Heat slowly, stirring constantly, *just* until sugar dissolves. Pour into a large bowl; chill until mixture is cold.
2 Stir in fudge topping, vanilla and remaining 5 cups cream. Pour into a 16-cup can of an electric or hand-crank ice-cream freezer. Freeze, following manufacturer's directions.
3 Unsnap cranking gear; carefully wipe cover and around side of can with a damp cloth. Lift off lid; remove dasher. Serve immediately. Or, to hard-freeze, repack, following manufacturer's directions; let stand about two hours. To store in your freezer, lift can from pail and wipe outside to remove all ice and salt; cover. Place in freezer until serving time.

Chocolate Ice Cream Supreme
Makes about 2 quarts

1 cup milk
¼ cup dry cocoa (not a mix)
3 cups cream for whipping

¼ cup finely chopped sweet cooking chocolate
6 egg yolks
1 cup sugar

1 Gradually add milk to cocoa in a medium-size saucepan; mixing until well blended; add cream; heat slowly just until bubbles appear around edge. Stir in chocolate until melted.
2 Beat egg yolks until frothy in small bowl of mixer; gradually add sugar, beating until fluffy-thick. Stir a small portion of hot mixture into egg yolks; add to hot mixture in saucepan. Cook, stirring constantly, over low heat until mixture thickens slightly and coats a spoon. Strain into an 8-cup can of an electric or hand-crank ice cream freezer. Chill until ready to freeze.
3 Freeze, following manufacturer's directions.
4 Unsnap cranking gear, carefully wipe cover and around side of can with a damp cloth; remove dasher. Spoon ice cream into serving dishes. If you prefer ice cream hard-frozen, repack following manufacturer's directions and let stand about 2 hours.

Milk-Chocolate Mousse
Each luscious spoonful just coaxes you into having more. As a party dessert it's a perfect make-ahead choice.
Makes 8 servings

1 package (6 ounces) semisweet-chocolate pieces
⅓ cup water

½ cup sugar
⅛ teaspoon salt
2 eggs, separated
1 teaspoon vanilla
2 cups cream for whipping
CANDIED ORANGE SLICES (recipe follows)

1 Combine chocolate pieces and water in a small saucepan; heat very slowly, stirring constantly, until chocolate melts and mixture is smooth. Stir in ¼ cup of the sugar and salt; heat, stirring constantly, until sugar dissolves; remove from heat.
2 Beat egg yolks slightly in a small bowl; very slowly beat in hot chocolate mixture and vanilla; cool.
3 Beat egg whites until foamy-white and double in volume in a medium-size bowl; beat in remaining ¼ cup sugar, 1 tablespoon at a time, until meringue stands in firm peaks. Beat cream until stiff in a second medium-size bowl.
4 Fold cooled chocolate mixture into meringue, then fold in whipped cream until no streaks of white remain. Pour into an 8-inch springform pan; cover.
5 Freeze six hours, or until firm.
6 When ready to serve, loosen dessert around edge with a knife; release spring and carefully lift off side of pan. Place dessert, still on its metal base, on a serving plate. Garnish top and side

Milk-Chocolate Mousse is a make-ahead party dessert.

Everyone's summer favorite—hand cranked ice cream.

with CANDIED ORANGE SLICES. Cut in wedges.

CANDIED ORANGE SLICES—Cut a small seedless orange into 12 thin slices; halve each. Sprinkle ½ cup sugar on a large plate; place orange slices in a single layer on top. Let stand at room temperature, turning two or three times, 2 hours, or until glazed. Remove and place on wax paper to dry slightly.

Frozen Strawberry Mallo
Makes 6 servings

1 package frozen sliced strawberries, thawed
1 cup (8-ounce container) dairy sour cream
½ teaspoon lemon peel
1 tablespoon lemon juice
1 cup small-size marshmallows or cut-up regular size

1 Mash strawberries with a fork in large bowl; add sour cream, lemon peel and juice; mix well; fold in marshmallows.
2 Pour into ice-cube tray; freeze about 2 hours, or until firm.

Strawberry-Pink Mousse
Berries and cream—through and through—make this favorite frozen dessert.
Makes 6 servings

1 pint strawberries, washed and hulled
½ cup sugar
1 tablespoon lemon juice
1½ cups cream for whipping

1 Set aside a few whole berries for garnish. Press remaining through a sieve; mix with sugar and lemon juice in a medium-size bowl.
2 Beat cream until stiff in a medium-size bowl; fold into strawberry mixture; spoon into 2 ice-cube trays. Freeze until firm about 1 inch in from edges.
3 Stir until smooth; pour into a 5-cup mold or bowl. Freeze again until firm.
4 When ready to serve, loosen mold around edge with a knife; dip *very quickly* in and out of a pan of hot water; invert onto serving plate. Garnish with saved strawberries and more whipped cream, if you wish.

1804

Frozen Strawberry Soufflé
It's a creamy spectacular with a soft pink collar that stands handsomely high.
Makes 12 servings

6 cups (3 pints) strawberries, washed
6 eggs, separated
1½ cups sugar
¼ teaspoon red food coloring
1 cup sugar (for meringue)
¼ teaspoon cream of tartar
½ cup water
3 cups cream for whipping
3 tablespoons ready-to-eat high-protein cereal

1 Fold a piece of aluminum foil, 12 inches wide and long enough to go around an 8-cup baking dish and overlap slightly, in thirds lengthwise. Wrap around dish to make a 2-inch stand-up collar; hold in place with a rubber band and a paper clip.
2 Save 3 perfect strawberries for topping; hull remaining and press through a sieve with a fork or crush in an electric blender (you should have 2¼ cups.)
3 Beat egg yolks (save whites for Step 5) with 1½ cups sugar and red food coloring in top of small double boiler. Stir in 1½ cups strawberry purée (save remaining ¾ cup for Step 6). Cook over simmering water, stirring often, 15 minutes, or until mixture thickens. Remove top from heat and let cool until Step 6.
4 Combine 1 cup sugar, cream of tartar and water in small heavy saucepan. Heat slowly, stirring constantly, until sugar is dissolved, then cook rapidly, without stirring, to 240° on candy thermometer (a spoonful of syrup will form a soft ball in cold water).
5 While syrup cooks, beat egg whites until they form soft peaks in a large bowl. *Gradually* pour hot syrup over in a thin stream, beating constantly, until meringue stands in firm peaks. Set bowl in a larger bowl of ice cubes to cool slightly.
6 Beat cream until stiff in large bowl. Fold in cooled strawberry mixture and remaining ¾ cup puréed strawberries, then fold in cooled meringue until no streaks of white remain. Carefully spoon into prepared dish; freeze until firm or overnight.
7 To serve, garnish with cereal and whole berries; remove foil collar.

Frosty Fruit Cream
Simplest way we know to make homemade fruit ice cream.
Makes 6 servings

Crispy store-bought sugar wafers give Maple Butter-Nut Charlotte an elegant and decorative flourish.

1 small can evaporated milk (⅔ cup)
1 package (10 ounces) frozen red raspberries
  or sliced strawberries, thawed
½ cup sugar
  Pinch of salt
2 tablespoons lemon juice

1 Pour milk into freezer tray; chill 5 to 10 minutes, or until frozen about 1 inch in from edge.
2 Crush fruit in small bowl; stir in sugar and salt until dissolved.
3 Beat chilled milk until stiff in medium-size bowl; beat in lemon juice; fold in fruit mixture.
4 Pour into freezer tray; cover with wax paper or aluminum foil. Freeze about 3 hours, or until firm.

Raspberry Mousse
Makes 6 to 8 servings

2 packages frozen red raspberries, thawed
1 cup cream for whipping
⅔ cup 10X (confectioners' powdered) sugar
⅛ teaspoon salt
¼ cup cream, whipped (for topping)

1 Save 3 raspberries for garnish; press remaining through sieve into medium-size bowl.
2 Beat 1 cup cream until foamy in second bowl; add sugar and salt; beat until stiff; gently fold into sieved raspberries; spoon into dry ice-cube tray.
3 Freeze until ice crystals form around edge; stir until smooth; spoon into a 4-cup fancy mold or bowl; freeze until firm.
4 To unmold; Loosen around edge with small spatula; dip mold or bowl *very quickly* into hot water; set serving plate on top; turn upside down; lift off mold; garnish with whipped cream and raspberries.

Maple Butter-Nut Charlotte
Crispy sugar wafers frame a delectably rich mousselike cream.
Makes 8 to 12 servings

1¼ cups butter-blended syrup
  3 egg whites
  2 cups cream for whipping
  2 teaspoons vanilla

¾ cup chopped walnuts
1 package (3 ounces) sugar wafers

1 Heat syrup to boiling in medium-size saucepan; boil 3 minutes.
2 Beat egg whites until they stand in firm peaks in medium-size bowl. Beating constantly, *gradually* pour in hot syrup in a thin stream; continue beating about 5 minutes, or until syrup mixture is cool. (Mixture will be liquid, not fluffy like meringue.)
3 Beat 1½ cups cream and vanilla until stiff in large bowl. (Save remaining cream for Step 5.) Gradually fold in cooled syrup mixture, then walnuts.
4 Stand sugar wafers, about ½ inch apart, around side of a 7-inch spring-form pan; lay remaining wafers on bottom. Spoon in cream mixture; freeze 4 hours, or until firm.
5 Beat saved ½ cup cream until stiff in small bowl; spread over top; decorate with walnut halves, if you wish. Freeze until serving time.
6 Release spring and lift off side of pan; place charlotte on serving plate. Cut into wedge-shape pieces.

Orange Blossom Ice Cream
Top this tangy-sweet frosty with sparkling rivulets of burnt-sugar sauce.
Makes 6 to 8 servings

1¼ cups milk
⅔ cup sugar
1 can (6 ounces) frozen concentrated orange juice
1 cup cream for whipping
⅛ teaspoon salt
1 tablespoon lemon juice
1 egg white, stiffly beaten
BURNT-SUGAR SAUCE *(recipe follows)*

1806

1 Combine milk and sugar in medium-size saucepan; heat, stirring constantly, just until sugar is dissolved. Remove from heat.
2 Stir in frozen orange juice, cream, salt and lemon juice. (Mixture will look curdled, but flecks will disappear when frozen.)
3 Pour into pan, 8x8x2, or 2 ice-cube trays; freeze until firm about 1 inch in from edge. Spoon into chilled large bowl; beat quickly until fluffy-smooth; fold in beaten egg white.
4 Return to pan; freeze 30 minutes; stir again. Freeze 2 to 3 hours longer, or until firm.
5 Spoon into sherbet glasses; pour BURNT-SUGAR SAUCE over.

BURNT-SUGAR SAUCE—Heat 1½ cups sugar in medium-size heavy frying pan or saucepan, stirring constantly with a wooden spoon, until melted into a golden syrup; remove from heat. Stir in 1 cup boiling water *very slowly*. (Watch it, as mixture will splatter.) Return to heat; cook, stirring constantly, until sugar mixture is smooth and syrupy. (Sauce will be thin, but will thicken as it cools.) Makes about 2 cups.
Note: Store any left over in a covered jar; reheat by setting jar in a pan of hot water for a few minutes.

Brandied Peach Ice Cream
Makes about 2 quarts

4 medium-size peaches, peeled, pitted and diced (about 2 cups)
¼ cup brandy
3 cups cream for whipping
1 cup sugar

1 Toss peaches with brandy in a large bowl; mash slightly.
2 Combine 1 cup of the cream with sugar in a small saucepan; heat slowly, stirring constantly, until sugar dissolves. Pour over peach mixture; stir in remaining 2 cups cream.
3 Pour into 8-cup can of an electric or hand-crank ice-cream freezer; freeze, following manufacturer's directions.
4 Unsnap cranking gear; carefully wipe cover and around side of can with damp cloth. Lift off lid; remove dasher. To hard-freeze ice cream, repack, following manufacturer's directions; let stand about 2 hours. Or, to store in your freezer, lift can from pail and wipe outside to remove all ice and salt; cover. Place in freezer until serving time.

Frozen Grape-Cream Cups
Makes 8 servings

3 tablespoons ready-to-eat high-protein cereal
1 can (6 ounces) frozen concentrate for grape-lemon punch
¾ cup sugar
2 cups cream for whipping
Candy violets

1 Prepare 8 straight-side demitasses this way; Cut strips of foil twice the depth of cups and long enough to wrap around with a 1-inch overlap; cut out notches to fit around cup handles.

Butter strips lightly; wrap each around a cup, buttered side in, to form a 1½-inch stand-up collar; hold in place with a paper clip and rubber band.

2 Sprinkle about 1 teaspoon cereal in each cup, turning cup on side and rolling to coat buttered collar well.

3 Thaw punch by running hot water over can for a few minutes; open and stir into sugar in a medium-size bowl until sugar dissolves.

4 Beat cream until stiff in a second medium-size bowl; fold into punch mixture until no streaks of white remain. Spoon into prepared cups, dividing evenly. Freeze several hours, or until firm.

5 To serve, remove paper clips and rubber bands and carefully peel off foil; sprinkle a little more cereal around sides. Garnish each with a candy violet.

Note: You can use small buttered cereal-coated molds for this dessert, if you wish. After freezing, unmold into dessert dishes and sprinkle with more cereal.

Apple-Cinnamon Ice Cream
Makes 8 to 10 servings

2 medium-size tart apples, pared, quartered, cored and chopped (2 cups)
¼ cup finely chopped seedless raisins
½ cup firmly packed brown sugar
½ teaspoon ground cinnamon
¼ cup water
3 pints vanilla ice cream

1 Combine apples, raisins, brown sugar, cinnamon and water in a medium-size saucepan. Heat, stirring constantly, to boiling; cover. Simmer 20 minutes, or until apples are tender. Cool completely.

2 Soften ice cream slightly; spread in a freezer-proof dish, 9x9x2. Drop cooled apple mixture by spoonfuls on top; draw a knife through mixture to marble. Cover.

3 Freeze several hours until firm.

Biscuit Tortoni
Makes 6 servings

2 eggs, separated
½ cup sifted 10X (confectioners' powdered) sugar
1¼ teaspoon vanilla
½ teaspoon almond extract

Orange Blossom Ice Cream and Burnt-Sugar Sauce.

1 cup cream for whipping, whipped
⅓ cup drained and chopped maraschino cherries
¾ cup crushed macaroons

1 Beat egg yolks until light and fluffy. Add 10X sugar, 1 tablespoon at a time, beating well after each addition. Mix in vanilla and almond extract.
2 Beat egg whites until they stand in stiff peaks; fold into egg-yolk mixture. Fold in whipped cream. Stir in maraschino cherries and all but 3 tablespoonfuls of the macaroon crumbs.
3 Spoon into 4-ounce paper soufflé cups. Top with remaining crushed macaroons.
4 Freeze until firm.

Cranberry Tortoni
Makes 6 servings

½ cup evaporated milk
1 tablespoon lemon juice
8 marshmallows, cut up
1 can (9 ounces) pineapple tidbits
1 cup canned whole cranberry sauce
2 tablespoons graham cracker crumbs

1 Chill evaporated milk in freezing tray about 20 minutes; pour into chilled bowl; whip until it begins to thicken; add lemon juice; whip until very stiff.
2 Fold in marshmallows, pineapple and juice and cranberry sauce.
3 Return to freezing tray or divide among six 4-ounce aluminum-foil molds or paper soufflé cups; freeze until firm; garnish with graham cracker crumbs.

Parfait Amandes
Makes 8 servings

1808

1½ cups sugar
½ cup water
6 egg yolks
2 tablespoons crème de noyau liqueur
2 cups cream for whipping
1 can (5 ounces) toasted slivered almonds, chopped fine
¼ cup chopped maraschino cherries

1 Lightly butter an 8-cup mold. Line mold with foil, leaving a 2-inch overhang all around; press foil smoothly against side of mold.
2 Combine sugar and water in a small saucepan; heat, stirring constantly, until sugar dis-

solves, then cook rapidly, without stirring, to 236° on a candy thermometer. (A teaspoonful of syrup will form a soft ball when dropped in cold water.)
3 Beat egg yolks until fluffy-light in a medium-size bowl. Beating constantly, pour in hot syrup in a thin steady stream; continue beating until mixture is very light and thick; cool slightly. Beat in liqueur. Chill until cold.
4 Beat cream until stiff in a medium-size bowl. Fold into chilled egg mixture; fold in almonds and cherries; spoon into prepared mold. Fold foil over top. Freeze several hours, or overnight, until very firm.
5 When ready to serve, peel back foil from top of mold. Pull up on foil to loosen around edge. Invert onto a serving plate; peel off foil. Garnish plate with whole maraschino cherries with stems, if you wish. Cut into slices with a sharp knife.

Frozen Eggnog Cheese Squares
For variety, simply chill dessert until set instead of freezing it.
Makes 8 to 12 servings

2 cups sugar cookie crumbs
4 tablespoons (½ stick) butter or margarine
1½ cups bottled eggnog
1 package vanilla-flavor whipped-dessert mix
3 cartons (4 ounces each) whipped cream cheese

1 Blend cookie crumbs and butter or margarine in a medium-size bowl; press half over bottom of a pan, 9x9x2.
2 Combine eggnog and whipped-dessert mix in a small deep bowl; beat, following label directions. Slowly beat in cream cheese until well blended.
3 Pour half into prepared pan; sprinkle with remaining crumb mixture; top with remaining cheese mixture.
4 Freeze 3 hours, or until firm. Cut into squares.

Pineapple Sherbet in Orange Cups
Makes 6 servings

2 cups buttermilk
1 can (6 ounces) frozen concentrated pineapple juice, thawed

1 cup sugar
6 small oranges, peeled
6 whole strawberries, washed and hulled

1 Combine buttermilk, pineapple juice and sugar in medium-size bowl; beat until well blended.
2 Pour into ice-cube tray, or pan, 8x8x2; freeze until firm almost to middle.
3 Spoon into chilled medium-size bowl; beat until fluffy-smooth. Return to tray; freeze 2 to 3 hours longer, or until firm.
4 Separate sections of each orange slightly to form a cup; place in dessert dishes. Scoop sherbet into center; garnish each with a fresh strawberry.

"Instant" Peach-Orange Sherbet
Makes 3 servings

1 package (10 ounces) frozen sliced peaches
1 tablespoon orange-flavor instant breakfast drink

1 Break apart frozen sliced peaches with a fork. Spoon into electric-blender container. Add orange-flavor instant breakfast drink.
2 Start blender at slow speed, beat about 15 seconds; turn off; stir with rubber spatula; turn to high speed and continue alternate beating and stirring about 3 minutes, or *just* until fruit is the consistency of sherbet.
3 Serve immediately or keep frozen in ice cube tray.

Buttermilk-Lime Sherbet
Makes 6 servings

4 cups buttermilk
1 cup sugar
1½ cups light corn syrup
1½ teaspoons grated lime peel
1½ teaspoons grated lemon peel
½ cup lime juice

1 Combine buttermilk and sugar in a large bowl; stir until sugar is completely dissolved. Blend in corn syrup, lime and lemon peels and lime juice.
2 Pour into 2 dry ice-cube trays; freeze until firm about 1 inch around edges. Stir until smooth; freeze until firm.

Lemon Snow Sherbet
This delicately light dessert is a perfect top-off to a bountiful dinner.
Makes 8 cups

4 cups buttermilk
1 cup sugar
1½ cups light corn syrup
1 tablespoon grated lemon peel
½ cup lemon juice

1 Combine all ingredients in a large bowl; stir until sugar is dissolved.
2 Pour into 2 dry ice-cube trays; freeze until firm about 1 inch around edges; stir until smooth; freeze until firm.

Italian Ice
Makes 4 to 6 servings

3 cups water
¾ cup sugar
1 can (6 ounces) frozen concentrated pineapple-orange juice

1 Simmer water and sugar 5 minutes; stir in and melt frozen concentrated pineapple-orange juice.
2 Freeze in freezer tray until mushy-firm. Serve in small paper cups; squeeze cup from bottom or use a spoon.

Grape Ice
Makes 4 to 6 servings

2¼ cups water
¼ cup light corn syrup
¾ cup sugar
1 can (6 ounces) frozen concentrated grape juice
1 tablespoon lemon juice

1 Simmer water, light corn syrup and sugar 5 minutes; stir in and melt frozen concentrated grape juice. Stir in lemon juice.
2 Freeze in freezer tray until mushy-firm. Serve in small paper cups; squeeze cup from bottom or use a spoon.

Cranberry Ice
Makes 4 to 6 servings

2¼ cups cranberry juice cocktail
¼ cup light corn syrup

1809

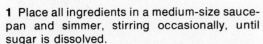

½ cup sugar
2 tablespoons lemon juice

1 Place all ingredients in a medium-size saucepan and simmer, stirring occasionally, until sugar is dissolved.
2 Freeze in freezer tray until mushy-firm. Serve in small paper cups; squeeze cup from bottom or use a spoon.

Watermelon Ice
Makes 4 servings

3 cups small pieces watermelon, seeded
2 tablespoons lemon juice
½ cup sugar
1 envelope unflavored gelatin
½ cup water

1 Place watermelon, about half at a time, in an electric-blender container; cover. Beat until smooth and liquid. (There should be about 2 cups.) Pour into a medium-size bowl; stir in lemon juice. (If you do not have a blender, press watermelon through a sieve into a bowl.)
2 Mix sugar and gelatin in a small saucepan; stir in water. Heat slowly, stirring constantly, until gelatin dissolves. Cool slightly; stir into watermelon mixture. Pour into a pan, 9x9x2.
3 Freeze about 1½ hours, or until firm around edges.
4 Spoon into a large bowl; beat until smooth; return to pan. Freeze several hours longer, or until firm.

SOME QUICK VARIATIONS ON STORE-BOUGHT ICE CREAMS AND SHERBETS

Spumoni
With store-bought ice cream and a few extras, you can whip up this Italian fancy at home in a short time.
Makes 8 to 10 servings

1810

1 can (5 ounces) slivered blanched almonds
1 tablespoon butter or margarine
½ teaspoon salt
2 pints vanilla ice cream
1 pint coffee ice cream
1 pint strawberry ice cream
1 cup cream for whipping
2 tablespoons sugar
Red food coloring

1 Spread almonds in a large shallow baking pan. Heat in moderate oven (350°) 10 minutes, or until lightly toasted; set aside a few for garnish, if you wish, then toss remaining with butter

or margarine and salt to coat evenly. Cool; chop coarsely.
2 Line an 8-cup bowl with foil or wax paper, allowing a 2-inch overhang.
3 Spoon vanilla ice cream into a medium-size bowl; stir to soften, then stir in chopped almonds; pack into lined bowl, shaping around edge to leave a hollow in middle.
4 Repeat with coffee ice cream to make a middle layer, then strawberry ice cream to fill center. Smooth top even; fold foil or wax paper over top to cover. Freeze until just before serving time.
5 Beat cream with sugar and a few drops food coloring until stiff in a medium-size bowl.
6 Peel paper from top of ice-cream mold; invert ice cream onto a serving plate; lift off bowl and peel off paper. Frost mold with tinted whipped cream; sprinkle with saved almonds. Cut mold into wedges with a thin sharp-blade knife.

Holiday Ice Cream
Makes 6 servings

2 pints vanilla ice cream
1 cup mincemeat, well chilled

1 Place ice cream in large chilled bowl; break up with fork and beat until creamy but not melted. Stir in mincemeat.
2 Pour into 2 refrigerator trays; freeze 1 to 2 hours, or until ice cream is firm enough to serve.

Ice-Cream Fluff
The youngsters will love this new way to vary ice cream. Note how it stretches the servings from just one pint.
Makes 6 servings

1 envelope unflavored gelatin
½ cup cold water
2 instant sparkling-drink tablets (any flavor)
1 pint vanilla ice cream, slightly softened

1 Soften gelatin in cold water in small saucepan; heat, stirring constantly, until gelatin is dissolved.
2 Remove from heat; add instant sparkling-drink tablets; mix until dissolved; beat in ice cream; spoon into 6 serving dishes; chill until serving time.

Double Orange Coupe
Scalloped orange shells hold frosty sherbet flavored with Cointreau. For festive serving, nestle each in crushed ice.
Makes 8 servings

8 large seedless oranges
3 pints orange sherbet
6 tablespoons Cointreau
   Crushed Ice
   Mint

1 Cut a thin slice from stem end of each orange. Run a small sharp-tip knife around inside of rind to loosen fruit. (Be careful not to puncture rind.) Cut fruit in big pieces and lift out; chill to serve for breakfast another day.
2 With a knife or pencil, mark scallops all around top edges of orange shells; trim around marks with a knife. Place cups in a shallow pan in freezer.
3 Beat sherbet just until softened in a large bowl; beat in Cointreau.
4 Spoon into orange shells, mounding slightly. Freeze again until firm.
5 When ready to serve, place crushed ice in 8 sherbet glasses; stand an orange cup in each. Garnish with a sprig of mint.

Celebration Fruit Sherbet
Makes 4 servings

1 pint orange sherbet
1 can (about 10 ounces) mandarin oranges, drained
1 can (about 9 ounces) pineapple tidbits, drained
½ cup bottled raspberry syrup

1 Scoop sherbet into 4 dessert dishes.
2 Arrange few pieces each of the oranges and pineapple on wooden picks; press into the sherbet; spoon remainder around edge. Freeze until serving time.
3 Just before serving, spoon raspberry syrup over.

SUNDAES, SPLITS, ALASKAS AND OTHER FABULOUS FROZEN DESSERTS MADE FROM STORE-BOUGHT ICE CREAMS

Hot Fudge Sundaes
Makes 4 to 6 servings

1 quart vanilla ice cream
1 recipe HOT FUDGE SAUCE (see recipe index for page number)
½ cup chopped pecans or walnuts (optional)

1 Using a No. 30 ice cream scoop or shaping ice cream into balls with two teaspoons, pile 4 to 5 small balls of ice cream in each of 4 to 6 dessert dishes.
2 Ladle HOT FUDGE SAUCE on top and, if you like, sprinkle with chopped pecans or walnuts.

VARIATIONS:

Double Fudge Sundaes—Prepare as directed for HOT FUDGE SUNDAES but substitute chocolate ice cream for vanilla.
Mocha Fudge Sundaes—Prepare as directed for HOT FUDGE SUNDAES but substitute coffee ice cream for vanilla.
Berry Fudge Sundaes—Prepare as directed for HOT FUDGE SUNDAES but substitute strawberry or raspberry ice cream for vanilla.
Cherry Fudge Sundaes—Prepare as directed for HOT FUDGE SUNDAES but substitute cherry ice cream for vanilla.
Chocolate Mint Sundaes—Prepare as directed for HOT FUDGE SUNDAES but substitute peppermint or mint ice cream for vanilla.

Regal Rio Sundaes
Double chocolate and doubly rich—that's what these easy-make sundae splurges are.
Count on 1 quart of ice cream for 6 to 8 servings. Scoop into dessert dishes; pour warm RIO CHOCOLATE SAUCE over; stand a CHOCOLATE FAN on top of each. (Recipes follow.)

Rio Chocolate Sauce
Makes 2 cups

1 cup (6-ounce package) semisweet-chocolate pieces
4 tablespoons (½ stick) butter or margarine
1 cup sifted 10X (confectioners' powdered) sugar
½ cup light corn syrup
1 teaspoon instant coffee powder
   Dash of salt
½ cup hot water
1 teaspoon vanilla

1 Melt chocolate pieces with butter or margarine in top of double boiler over simmering water. Beat in remaining ingredients until smooth and slightly thickened. Remove from heat.

2 Serve warm or cold over ice cream or pudding or cake desserts. (Make enough to keep on hand, as it stays creamy-smooth stored in a covered jar in the refrigerator. To reheat, set jar, covered, in a pan of simmering water; heat slowly for 10 to 15 minutes.)

Chocolate Fans
Makes 8 fans

Melt ½ cup (half a 6-ounce package) semi-sweet-chocolate pieces with 1 teaspoon vegetable shortening in top of small double boiler over hot, *not boiling,* water. Pour onto a foil-lined cookie sheet; spread evenly into a thin rectangle about 12x6. Chill 15 minutes, or just until beginning to be firm but not hard. Press 3-inch round cutter into chocolate to make 8 circles, then trim each to form a fan shape. Chill again until chocolate is firm. Carefully peel off foil and lift out fans with knife and small spatula. (Eat the trimmings as candy or break up and sprinkle over sundae.

Brownie Sundae Shortcakes
Brownie dough-in-a-roll from the dairy case stars in this quick dessert.
Bake at 375° for 30 minutes. Makes 6 servings

1 roll refrigerated fudge brownies
2 pints chocolate-ripple ice cream
  Creamy topping from a pressurized can

1 Press fudge brownies into a baking pan, 8x8x2, following label directions.
2 Bake in moderate oven (375°) 30 minutes, or until top is firm when lightly pressed with fingertip. Cut into 12 bars.
3 Put each 2 together with ice cream between on a serving plate; top with creamy topping from a pressurized can.

Peppermint Fudge Sundaes
Makes 6 servings

2 pints vanilla ice cream
1 package (6 ounces) semisweet-chocolate pieces
½ cup light corn syrup
1 tablespoon butter or margarine
1 teaspoon vanilla
½ cup crushed pink peppermint-stick candy
6 small pink peppermint sticks

1 Shape ice cream into 6 balls with ice-cream scoop or 2 tablespoons; place in ice-cube trays in freezing unit until ready to serve.
2 While ice cream chills, combine semi-sweet-chocolate pieces, corn syrup and butter or margarine in top of double boiler; heat over hot water, stirring often, until chocolate melts and sauce is smooth; stir in vanilla; cool slightly.
3 Spoon fudge sauce into bottom of serving dishes; place ice-cream ball on top; sprinkle with crushed candy; poke a candy stick in top. Pass remaining sauce.

Chocolate Skyscrapers
Makes 6 servings

¼ cup semisweet-chocolate pieces (from a 6-ounce package)
1 teaspoon vegetable shortening
1 can (about 4 ounces) flaked coconut
3 pints ice cream
  Chocolate syrup

1 Combine chocolate pieces and shortening in the top of a small double boiler; heat over hot water until melted; remove from heat. Stir in coconut until evenly coated.
2 Divide mixture among 6 buttered medium-size muffin-pan cups; press against sides and bottoms of cups to form shells. Chill at least 2 hours, or until firm.
3 Just before serving, run the tip of a knife around shells to loosen; turn out onto serving plates.
4 Scoop ice cream into shells; top each with chocolate sauce.

Lace-Wafer Sundaes
Perch a delicately crisp tissue-thin wafer atop each sundae to nibble separately or to shatter over its sparkling sauce.

Allow 1 quart ice cream for 6 to 8 servings. Shape into small balls; place 2 in each dessert dish. Pour warm CARAMEL SUNDAE SAUCE over; top each serving with a LACE WAFER. (Both recipes follow). Pass the rest for seconds.

Caramel Sundae Sauce
It's delectably sweet and clear as crystal.
Makes 1 cup.

Melt 1½ cups sugar in a small heavy frying pan, stirring constantly with wooden spoon, just until sugar is golden. Stir in ½ cup boiling water *very slowly* (watch it, as mixture will splatter). Cook about 3 minutes, or until a teaspoon of syrup

1813

Regal Rio Sundaes take commercial vanilla ice cream, homemade coffee-spiked sauce and chocolate fans.

dropped into cold water forms a soft ball (238° on candy thermometer). Serve warm.

Lace Wafers
They literally melt in your mouth, they're so crisp and buttery.
Bake at 350° for 5 to 6 minutes. Makes 20 cookies

  4 tablespoons (½ stick) butter or margarine
¼ cup sugar
1½ teaspoons all-purpose flour
  1 tablespoon cream
⅓ cup finely chopped blanched almonds

1 Melt butter or margarine in small saucepan; stir in remaining ingredients; remove from heat.
2 Drop batter by teaspoonfuls, 3 inches apart, on well-buttered cookie sheet; spread each into a 2-inch round. (Make only 4 to 6 wafers at a time so they do not touch.)
3 Bake in moderate oven (350°) 5 to 6 minutes, or just until light golden; cool on cookie sheet only 2 to 3 minutes, or until firm enough to remove with spatula; cool completely on wire racks. (If cookies become too brittle to remove easily, return cookie sheet to oven for 30 seconds to soften them.)
4 Bake remaining cookies on same sheet. No need to wash or re-butter.

Kona Sundaes
Makes 8 servings

¾ cup firmly packed light brown sugar
  1 tablespoon instant coffee powder
    Dash of salt
½ cup water
  1 can (15 ounces) sweetened condensed milk
  3 pints vanilla or coffee ice cream

1 Mix brown sugar, instant coffee, salt and water in medium-size heavy saucepan; heat, stirring constantly, to boiling, then cook, without stirring, to 230° on a candy thermometer. (A little syrup will spin fine threads when dropped from tip of spoon.) Remove from heat.
2 Place sweetened condensed milk (*not evaporated milk*) in medium-size bowl; blend in hot syrup slowly; cool.
3 When ready to serve, scoop ice cream into dessert dishes, dividing evenly; spoon sauce over.

Coffee-Almond Sparkle Sundaes
Makes 6 servings.

  2 cups firmly packed brown sugar
¼ cup dark corn syrup
  3 tablespoons water
  1 tablespoon lemon juice
¾ teaspoon salt
  1 tablespoon butter or margarine
  1 teaspoon vanilla
  2 pints coffee ice cream
¼ cup toasted blanched almonds

1 Mix sugar, corn syrup, water, lemon juice and salt in medium-size saucepan. Heat slowly, stirring just until sugar dissolves; add butter or margarine.
2 Heat to boiling; cook, without stirring, to 230° on candy thermometer. (A little syrup will spin fine threads when dropped from tip of spoon.)
3 Remove from heat; stir in vanilla; cool.
4 Scoop ice cream into dessert dishes; spoon sauce over; top with almonds.

Sinker Sundaes
Makes 6 servings

½ cup crunchy peanut butter
½ cup light corn syrup
¼ cup water
  6 plain doughnuts
  1 pint vanilla ice cream

1 Combine peanut butter with corn syrup and water in a small saucepan; heat slowly, stirring constantly, until well blended; cool.
2 For each sundae, place a doughnut in a serving dish; top with ice cream; drizzle with warm peanut sauce.

Quick Butterscotch Sundaes
Makes 6 servings

1½ cups firmly packed light brown sugar
½ cup light corn syrup
  1 tablespoon butter or margarine
  1 small can (⅔ cup) evaporated milk
½ teaspoon vanilla
  1 quart vanilla ice cream

1 Boil brown sugar and corn syrup, stirring often, 5 minutes. Add butter or margarine, pour into a bowl and cool 10 minutes.
2 Slowly stir in evaporated milk and vanilla. Spoon warm over vanilla ice cream.

1814

Honey-Butter Sundaes
Makes 4 servings

½ cup honey
1 tablespoon butter or margarine
3 tablespoons orange juice
½ teaspoon vanilla
¼ teaspoon almond extract
1 quart vanilla ice cream

1 Heat honey, butter or margarine and orange juice in a small saucepan about 5 minutes, stirring often.
2 Remove from heat, stir in vanilla and almond extract. Cool about 5 minutes; spoon warm over vanilla ice cream.

Bunny Sundaes
Makes 4 servings

½ pound caramel-candy cubes
½ cup evaporated milk
4 marshmallows
   Red food coloring
8 small red gumdrops
1 pint coffee ice cream

1 Melt caramels in milk over hot water, stirring often to blend.
2 Draw bunny face on marshmallows with wooden pick and food coloring; attach gumdrop "ears" with picks.
3 Spoon caramel sauce over each serving of ice cream; top with marshmallow bunny.

Banana Splits Royale
For each serving, arrange 1 scoop each strawberry, chocolate and peppermint ice cream* in oval or round dessert dish. Top strawberry ice cream with sweetened crushed strawberries (fresh or frozen kind, thawed); chocolate ice cream with MARSHMALLOW SAUCE and semisweet-chocolate pieces; peppermint ice cream with CHOCOLATE SUNDAE SAUCE and chopped walnuts. (See recipe index for page numbers of sauce recipes). Slice 1 peeled banana lengthwise, then crosswise into 4 sticks; stand, fan-shape, behind ice creams; garnish front with whipped cream and whole strawberries.

* 1 pint each strawberry, chocolate and peppermint ice cream makes 3 to 4 servings.

Christmas Eggnog Sundae Ring
Festive and rich-as-can-be dessert—a recipe your guests will want for their own files.
Makes 12 servings

3 pints pistachio ice cream
6 eggs
¾ cup sugar
2 cups half-and-half (milk and cream)
1 tablespoon rum extract
1 cup cream, whipped
   Fresh or frozen strawberries

1 Form ice cream into 12 large balls with a scoop or 2 spoons; place on a metal pan and freeze until firm. Pile balls into a medium-size bowl; freeze until ready to serve (freezing balls separately first helps to hold their shape and makes serving easier).
2 Separate eggs, putting yolks in large bowl, whites in medium-size one. Beat whites until foamy; add ¼ cup sugar, a tablespoon at a time, beating well after each addition, until meringue stands in stiff peaks.
3 Beat yolks until thick, beating in remaining ½ cup sugar; stir in half-and-half and rum extract.
4 Fold in whipped cream and meringue; chill until ready to serve.
5 Unmold ice-cream balls in middle of your prettiest large shallow serving bowl; pour in eggnog mixture; garnish with sliced strawberries.

1815

Calypso Sundaes
Makes 8 servings

1 can (about 1 pound) pear halves, drained
1 can (9 ounces) crushed pineapple
½ cup mint jelly
1 teaspoon lemon juice
2 pints lemon sherbet
   Maraschino cherries

1 Break up pear halves with spoon in medium-size saucepan; add pineapple and juice

Jubilee Sundae Stacks are literally made in a jiffy.

and mint jelly; simmer 10 minutes, or until blended and slightly thickened; add lemon juice; chill.
2 Spoon over sherbet in serving dishes; top with maraschino cherries.

Jubilee Sundae Stacks
Makes 4 servings

4 packaged dessert shells
1 pint vanilla ice cream
1 package (10 ounces) quick-thaw frozen dark
  sweet cherries

Place each dessert shell on a serving plate; top with a scoop of ice cream; spoon cherries over all.

Double Strawberry Sundaes
Makes 4 servings

2 tablespoons strawberry preserves
1 cup fresh strawberries, washed, hulled and
  halved

1816

1 pint vanilla ice cream
2 tablespoons frozen whipped dessert topping
12 pecan halves

1 Heat preserves very slowly until melted in a small saucepan. Pour over strawberries in a small bowl; toss lightly to coat berries. Let stand at least 30 minutes.
2 When ready to serve, spoon ice cream, dividing evenly, into 4 dessert dishes; top each with the glazed strawberries, then whipped topping and pecans.

Strawberry Sundae Pizza
Teens will get a kick out of this sweet twist on their favorite.
Bake at 400° for 12 minutes. Makes 8 to 12 servings

1 package piecrust mix
¼ cup sugar
1 egg, beaten
3 pints vanilla ice cream
1 package (10 ounces) frozen sliced strawberries, thawed
1 tablespoon cornstarch
2 tablespoons cold water
¼ cup semisweet-chocolate pieces (from a 6-
  ounce package)
1 teaspoon vegetable shortening

1 Combine piecrust mix and sugar in a medium-size bowl; stir in beaten egg to make a stiff dough.
2 Roll out to a 16-inch round on a lightly floured pastry cloth or board; fit into a 14-inch pizza pan; trim overhang to ½ inch; turn under, flush with rim; flute to make a stand-up edge. Prick well all over with a fork.
3 Bake in hot oven (400°) 12 minutes, or until pastry is golden; cool completely in pan on a wire rack.
4 Spoon ice cream, petal fashion, into cooled pastry shell; freeze until firm.
5 Heat strawberries slowly, mashing berries well with back of spoon, until bubbly-hot in a small saucepan.
6 Blend cornstarch with water until smooth in a cup; stir into hot strawberries. Cook, stirring constantly, until sauce thickens and boils 3 minutes; cool completely, then chill.
7 Melt chocolate pieces with shortening in a cup over simmering water; spread in a thin rectangle, 6x5, on a cookie sheet; chill until almost firm.
8 Cut into twenty ¼-inch-wide strips; roll each strip, jelly-roll fashion, using tip of knife; chill again until firm.
9 When ready to serve, spoon strawberry sauce

in rings on top of pizza; garnish with chocolate rolls. Cut into wedges.

●

Strawberry Sundae Cake

Bake cake, put together with its ice-cream fillings and frost a day ahead, then let your freezer do the rest.

Bake at 350° for 30 minutes. Makes 12 servings

1¼ cups sifted cake flour
 1 teaspoon baking powder
 ½ teaspoon salt
 ⅓ cup vegetable shortening
 1 cup sugar
 2 eggs
1½ teaspoons vanilla
 ½ cup milk
 2 pints vanilla ice cream, softened
 1 pint raspberry sherbet, softened
 2 cups cream for whipping
   STRAWBERRY TOPPING (recipe follows)

1 Grease a 9x1½-inch layer-cake pan; line bottom with wax paper; grease paper.
2 Sift flour, baking powder and salt onto another sheet of wax paper.
3 Cream shortening in a medium-size bowl; gradually beat in ¾ cup of the sugar until mixture is fluffy, then beat in eggs, one at a time, and ½ teaspoon of the vanilla. (Remaining ¼ cup sugar and 1 teaspoon vanilla are for Step 9.)
4 Add sifted flour mixture, a third at a time, alternately with milk, stirring just until blended; pour into prepared pan.
5 Bake in moderate oven (350°) 30 minutes, or until top springs back when lightly pressed with fingertip.
6 Cool cake in pan on wire rack 5 minutes. Loosen around edge with a knife; turn out onto rack; peel off wax paper; cool cake completely.
7 Split cake into three thin layers with a sharp knife; press bottom layer into an 8-inch spring-form pan. Spread with 1 pint of the vanilla ice cream; top with second layer; spread with all of the raspberry sherbet; top with third cake layer. Spread with remaining 1 pint vanilla ice cream.
8 Cover pan with transparent wrap; freeze several hours, or until very firm.
9 Beat cream with remaining ¼ cup sugar and 1 teaspoon vanilla until stiff.
10 Release spring from pan and carefully lift off side; place cake on a cookie sheet. Frost side and top with part of the whipped-cream mixture; spoon remaining in puffs around top edge to make a rim. Freeze overnight.
11 Prepare STRAWBERRY TOPPING and cool. Just before serving, place frozen cake on a serving plate; spoon STRAWBERRY TOPPING in center. Cut cake in wedges with a sharp knife.

STRAWBERRY TOPPING—Thaw 1 package (10 ounces) frozen sliced strawberries. Stir a little of the syrup into 2 tablespoons cornstarch until smooth in a small saucepan, then stir in remaining berries and syrup. Cook, stirring constantly, over low heat until sauce thickens and boils 3 minutes. Cool completely. Makes 1¼ cups.

Pink and White Angel Sundaes
Makes 6 servings

1 packaged round or loaf angel food cake
1 quart vanilla ice cream
1 recipe PINK PEPPERMINT SAUCE (see recipe index for page number)

1 Cut 6 thin wedges or slices of angel food cake and arrange on 6 dessert plates.
2 Place 2 scoops of ice cream on each cake wedge or slice and top with PINK PEPPERMINT SAUCE.

●

Peach Fiesta Splits
Makes 6 servings

1 package (10 ounces) frozen sliced peaches
½ teaspoon almond extract
1 pint vanilla ice cream
1 pint pistachio ice cream

1 Thaw peaches in a small bowl; stir in almond extract.
2 Scoop out vanilla and pistachio ice creams, dividing evenly among 6 dessert dishes. Spoon peaches on top.

Pear Splits
Makes 6 servings

12 canned pear halves
 1 quart vanilla ice cream
 1 recipe JIFFY FUDGE SAUCE (see recipe index for page number)
 ½ cup chopped salted peanuts

Arrange 2 pear halves in each of 6 dessert dishes. Place scoops of ice cream between pear halves, top with JIFFY FUDGE SAUCE and chopped peanuts.

1817

Peppermint Snowballs—a great way to beat the heat.

1-cup measure; tint delicate green with food coloring.
3 When ready to serve, pile sherbet balls into a pretty glass serving bowl; drizzle sauce over.

●

Chocolate Mint Parfaits

Creamy mint-flavored parfait mixture complemented by chocolate sauce is a treat that is unbelievably easy to make.
Makes 6 servings

1 pint vanilla ice cream
1 package (2 ounces) whipped topping mix
  Milk
1 envelope unflavored gelatin
⅓ cup water
1 teaspoon peppermint extract
  Green food coloring
½ cup bottled or canned chocolate sauce

1 Spoon ice cream into a large bowl and let stand at room temperature about 15 minutes, or until slightly softened.
2 Prepare topping mix with milk in a medium-size bowl, following label directions. Reserve ½ cup for garnish in Step 6.
3 Soften gelatin in water in a small saucepan, dissolve over low heat, stirring constantly; remove from heat.
4 With electric mixer, beat ice cream until smooth in a medium-size bowl; add peppermint extract and enough food coloring to tint a delicate green; fold in whipped topping. Add the hot gelatin all at once, beating in quickly and constantly, until mixture is smooth.
5 Layer mint mixture alternately with chocolate sauce into 6 parfait glasses.
6 Garnish each serving with reserved topping. Serve immediately or chill until serving time. Top with a sprig of fresh mint, if you wish.

●

Paradise Parfaits
Makes 8 servings

2 cups diced cantaloupe
1 cup red raspberries or sliced strawberries
3 pints strawberry ice cream
1 cup cream, whipped
4 peaches, peeled, halved and pitted

1 Layer fruits and ice cream, dividing evenly, into stemmed glasses this way: Cantaloupe, raspberries or strawberries, ice cream. Top each with whipped cream, then with a peach half.
2 Stick a perky Oriental paper parasol or lantern into each peach half, if you wish.

1818

Peppermint Snowballs
Makes 6 servings

2 pints lemon sherbet
½ cup light corn syrup
1½ teaspoons peppermint extract
  Green food coloring

1 Scoop lemon sherbet into balls with a small ice-cream scoop or shape with two spoons. Place on cookie sheet; cover loosely with wax paper, transparent wrap or foil; freeze until serving time.
2 Mix corn syrup and peppermint extract in a

DESSERTS MADE FROM STORE-BOUGHT ICE CREAMS

Tutti-Frutti Parfaits
Makes 6 servings

1 can (1 pound) fruit cocktail, drained
1 cup tiny marshmallows
1 cup (8-ounce carton) dairy sour cream
6 cup-shape ice-cream cones

1 Combine drained fruit cocktail, marshmallows and sour cream in medium-size bowl; stir lightly to mix.
2 Spoon into ice-cream cones; freeze several hours, or until firm.

Peachy Parfaits
Makes 8 servings

1 package (10 ounces) frozen sliced peaches, thawed
1 pint chocolate ice cream
CHOCOLATE VELVET SAUCE (see recipe index for page number)
1 pint pistachio ice cream
Whipped cream

Fill each of 8 chilled parfait glasses with a layer of peaches, chocolate ice cream, chocolate sauce and pistachio ice cream. Top with whipped cream and more peaches.

Cherry-Crème Parfaits
Makes 4 parfaits

1 cup cherry preserves
Few drops peppermint extract
½ cup cream, whipped
1 pint vanilla ice cream

1 Flavor cherry preserves with peppermint extract.
2 Spoon alternate layers of preserves, whipped cream and ice cream into parfait glasses; top with preserves.

Hazelnut Cream Bombe
Makes 12 to 16 servings

1 tablespoon butter or margarine
1 cup chopped hazelnuts or filberts
¼ cup candied green cherries, chopped
1½ pints vanilla ice cream, slightly softened
1 pint chocolate ice cream, slightly softened
1½ cups sugar
½ cup water
4 egg yolks
2 tablespoons light rum
3 cups cream for whipping

1 Melt butter or margarine in a shallow pan; sprinkle hazelnuts into pan, tossing to coat with butter. Toast in moderate oven (350°), stirring several times, 10 minutes, or until richly golden. Cool and set aside.
2 Lightly butter a 10-cup mixing bowl. Line with foil, pressing foil smooth against side and leaving a 2-inch overhang all around.
3 Stir cherries into vanilla ice cream in a medium-size bowl; spoon into foil-lined mold, shaping around edge to leave a hollow in middle. Freeze 2 hours, or until firm. Repeat with chocolate ice cream to make a thin middle layer; freeze.
4 While chocolate ice cream freezes, combine sugar and water in a medium-size saucepan. Cook rapidly to 236° on a candy thermometer. (A teaspoonful of syrup will form a soft ball when dropped in cold water.)
5 Beat egg yolks until fluffy-light in a medium-size bowl; slowly pour in syrup in a fine stream, beating constantly at high speed until mixture is very light and thick. Cool slightly; beat in rum. Chill until completely cold.

A mixing bowl is the mold for Hazelnut Cream Bombe.

6 Beat 2 cups of the cream until stiff in a medium-size bowl; fold into chilled egg mixture; fold in hazelnuts. Spoon into hollow in ice-cream mold; fold foil over top to cover. Freeze at least 6 hours, or overnight.

7 When ready to unmold, beat remaining 1 cup cream until stiff in a medium-size bowl.

8 Peel foil from top of mold; loosen around edge with a knife and pull up on foil to loosen from bowl. Invert onto a serving plate; peel off foil. Attach a rosette tip to a pastry bag; spoon whipped cream into bag. Press out in rows of rosettes, spoke fashion, around mold. To serve, cut in wedges.

Triple Cream Bombe

A mixing bowl is your mold for this simple but glamorous dessert.
Makes 6 to 8 servings

1 pint chocolate ice cream
1 pint vanilla ice cream
1 pint strawberry ice cream

1 Line a 6-cup bowl with slightly softened chocolate ice cream, shaping around edge to leave a hollow in middle; freeze until firm. Repeat with vanilla ice cream to make a middle layer, then strawberry ice cream to fill center; smooth top flat.

2 Cover bowl with double-thick foil or transparent wrap; freeze several hours, overnight, or until very firm.

3 When ready to serve, run a sharp-tip knife around top of mold to loosen, then dip *very quickly* in and out of a pan of hot water. Invert onto serving plate; lift off bowl. Garnish with almond slices and a maraschino cherry, if you wish. Cut in wedges.

Walnut Bombe Alaska

1820

Rush this beauty right from oven to table! Base is a rich cake topped with a mold of ice cream. Frosting is golden meringue.
Bake cake at 350° for 30 minutes, meringue at 475° for 3 to 4 minutes. Makes 12 servings

Ice-Cream Mold

2 pints coffee ice cream, slightly softened
1 pint strawberry ice cream, slightly softened

Torte Layer

1 cup sifted all-purpose flour
2 teaspoons baking powder
⅛ teaspoon salt
½ cup vegetable shortening
½ cup firmly packed brown sugar
4 egg yolks
⅓ cup milk
½ teaspoon vanilla
1 cup chopped walnuts

Meringue Frosting

4 egg whites
¼ teaspoon cream of tartar
½ cup sugar

1 Make ice-cream mold: Line an 8-cup melon mold or mixing bowl with foil, pressing it into the mold shape and leaving a 1-inch overhang all around. Spoon coffee ice cream into mold, spreading evenly over bottom and up side to line completely and leave a hollow in middle for strawberry ice cream. Freeze until firm, then spoon strawberry ice cream into hollow. Smooth top flat with a knife; cover. Freeze several hours, overnight, or until very firm.

2 Make torte layer: Measure flour, baking powder and salt into sifter.

3 Cream shortening with brown sugar until fluffy in a medium-size bowl; beat in egg yolks, 1 at a time, beating well after each addition until mixture is well blended.

4 Sift in dry ingredients, a third at a time, adding alternately with milk; stir just until blended, then stir in vanilla and walnuts. Pour into a greased and floured 9x1½-inch layer-cake pan.

5 Bake in moderate oven (350°) 30 minutes, or until top springs back when lightly pressed with fingertip.

6 Cool in pan on wire rack 5 minutes. Loosen around edge with knife; turn out onto rack; cool completely.

7 Put Alaska together this way: Place torte layer on a double-thick strip of foil on a cookie sheet. (This makes it easy to slide hot dessert onto its serving plate.) Loosen ice cream from mold by lifting up overhanging tabs of foil, then invert onto center of torte layer. Lift off mold; peel off foil. Trim torte layer to within ¼ inch of ice-cream mold. Return to freezer until ready to frost with meringue, bake, and serve.

8 Make meringue: Beat egg whites with cream of tartar until foamy-white and double in volume in a medium-size bowl. Sprinkle in granulated sugar *very slowly*, 1 tablespoon at a time, beating all the time until sugar completely dissolves and meringue stands in firm peaks. (Beating will take about 20 minutes in all.)

9 Spread over ice-cream-cake mold, swirling in peaks, to cover completely. (Work quickly so the ice cream doesn't melt.)

10 Bake in very hot oven (475°) 3 to 4 minutes, or just until peaks are toasty-golden.

11 Slide Alaska onto a chilled serving plate; pull out foil strip. Use a sharp bread or carving knife to slice or cut into wedges.

Walnut Bombe Alaska is a festive version of the "fire-and-ice" classic: two ice creams atop a walnut cake.

Note: To avoid last-minute fussing, you can frost ice-cream-cake mold with meringue ahead, then return to freezer. Just before serving, slide in to bake, following directions in Step 10 above.

Dublin Ice-Cream Bombe
Makes 10 servings

  1 quart coffee ice cream
  1 quart vanilla ice cream
  ½ cup Irish Mist liqueur
  1 teaspoon almond extract

1 Lightly butter an 8-cup bombe mold. Line mold with foil, leaving a 2-inch overhang all around; press foil smoothly against side of mold.
2 Soften coffee ice cream slightly in a medium-size bowl. Spoon into mold, smoothing over bottom and up side to make a shell about 1 inch thick. Freeze until firm.
3 Soften vanilla ice cream slightly in a medium-size bowl. Beat in liqueur and almond extract; spoon into center of mold; smooth top flat. Fold foil over top. Freeze several hours, or overnight, until very firm.
4 When ready to serve, peel back foil from top

of mold. Pull up on foil to loosen around edge. Invert onto a serving plate; peel off foil. Garnish with almonds, if you wish. Cut into slices with a sharp knife.

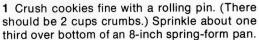

Mexican Cream Torte
Makes 6 to 8 generous servings

1 package (about 7 ounces) coconut cookies
3 pints chocolate ice cream, softened slightly
¾ cup chocolate syrup
1 pint orange sherbet, softened slightly
1 cup crushed peanut brittle

1 Crush cookies fine with a rolling pin. (There should be 2 cups crumbs.) Sprinkle about one third over bottom of an 8-inch spring-form pan.
2 Continue layering this way; Half of the chocolate ice cream, ¼ cup of the chocolate syrup, one third of the crumbs, orange sherbet, ¼ cup chocolate syrup, remaining crumbs, remaining chocolate ice cream and remaining syrup. Sprinkle peanut brittle over top.
3 Freeze at least 3 hours, or overnight.
4 When ready to serve, loosen torte around edge with a knife; release spring on pan and carefully lift off side. Slide torte, still on its metal base, onto a serving plate. Cut into wedges with a sharp knife.

Christmas Ice-Cream Log
This little beauty doesn't need a special mold. A clean empty juice can will do just fine.
Makes 8 to 10 servings

1 quart vanilla ice cream, slightly softened
½ cup chopped maraschino cherries
½ cup maraschino cherry juice
    Few drops red food coloring
1½ pints lemon sherbet, slightly softened
⅓ cup crème de menthe
1 cup cream for whipping
3 whole red maraschino cherries with stems
4 whole candied green cherries

1 Stir chopped cherries, cherry juice and red food coloring quickly into vanilla ice cream in a medium-size bowl. Using back of spoon or rubber scraper, press ice cream evenly around inside of a 46-ounce juice can (about ¾ inch thick). Freeze at least 2 hours, or until firm.
2 Stir crème de menthe quickly into lemon sherbet in a medium-size bowl; spoon into

center of can; cover with foil or transparent wrap. Freeze, in an upright position, at least 6 hours, or overnight.
3 Unmold one or two hours before serving. To unmold: Loosen around edge of mold with a sharp knife; dip mold, in an upright position, quickly into a large saucepan of hot water. Invert onto a plate; shake to loosen; remove mold. Turn the log on its side. Cover; return to freezer until surface is firm.
4 When ready to serve, beat the cream until stiff in a medium-size bowl. Remove stems from whole cherries; reserve. With a small sharp knife, cut maraschino cherries ¾ of the way down into 6 sections each, to make petals. Cut candied green cherries in half and place one half into the center of each of the 3 cherry flowers. Cut green leaves from the green candied cherries and reserve.
5 Attach a rosette tip to a pastry bag; spoon whipped cream into bag. Press out into rosettes along bottom and sides and top of ice cream log. Garnish with cherry flowers, leaves and stems. To serve, cut into slices.

Frozen Strawberry Crown
Ladyfingers frame a delectable mold of ice cream layered with strawberry sauce.
Makes 8 servings

2 pints strawberries, washed and hulled
1 cup sugar
8 ladyfingers, split
1 quart vanilla ice cream

1 Set aside 24 whole strawberries for garnish. Mash remaining in a medium-size saucepan; stir in sugar; heat to boiling. Cook, stirring often, 15 minutes; cool completely.
2 Butter a 6-inch spring-form pan. Stand ladyfingers, ¼ inch apart, around edge in pan; lay remaining in bottom. Spoon one third of the ice cream into pan; drizzle with ¼ cup sauce. Make two more layers of each, saving any remaining sauce; freeze.
3 When ready to serve, loosen dessert around edge with knife; remove side of pan. Place dessert, still on metal base, on a serving plate. Garnish with whole strawberries; drizzle with remaining sauce.

Coconut Cream Ring
Feathery lemon cake is split and filled, then frosted with billowy pink cream and coconut.
Makes 8 to 10 servings

1822

1 package lemon-chiffon cake mix
  Eggs
  Water
2 pints strawberry-ripple ice cream
1 cup cream for whipping
2 tablespoons 10X (confectioners' powdered)
  sugar
1 teaspoon vanilla
  Few drops red food coloring
¾ cup flaked coconut

1 Prepare cake mix with eggs and water, bake in a 10-inch angel-cake pan, cool, and remove from pan, following label directions. Wash pan; dry well.
2 Split cake crosswise into 3 even layers; return top layer to pan. (Set middle layer aside for another dessert.)
3 Spoon ice cream in an even layer over cake in pan; top with remaining cake layer; cover pan with transparent wrap or wax paper. Freeze several hours, or overnight.
4 About 2 hours before serving, beat cream with 10X sugar and vanilla until stiff in a medium-size bowl; fold in a few drops red food coloring to tint delicate pink.
5 Unmold cake onto a small cookie sheet. Frost with whipped cream; sprinkle top and side with coconut. Return to freezer.
6 About a half hour before serving, remove cake from freezer; place on a serving plate; let stand in refrigerator to soften for easy slicing. Cut into wedges with a sharp thin-blade knife, using a sawing motion.

Ribbon Ice-Cream Cake
Makes 12 to 16 servings

1 eight-inch dessert layer (2 to a package)
2 pints butter-pecan ice cream, softened
1 cup cream for whipping
1 square semisweet chocolate, grated
2 jars (12 ounces each) butterscotch ice-cream
  topping

1 Split dessert layer; place bottom half in an 8-inch spring-form pan. Spread with half of the ice cream; top with remaining dessert layer, then remaining ice cream, spreading evenly. Wrap pan in foil. Freeze at least 2 hours, or overnight.
2 Beat cream until stiff in a medium-size bowl; fold in chocolate. Loosen cake around edges with a knife; release spring and carefully lift off side of pan. Slide cake onto a freezerproof

Rainbow Ice-Cream Cake is a conversation piece.

serving plate; frost with whipped-cream mixture. Freeze 1 to 2 hours, or until firm.
3 Place jars of butterscotch topping in a pan of hot water to warm. Cut cake into wedges; place on serving plates. Spoon butterscotch topping over each.

Rainbow Ice-Cream Cake
Your freezer does all the work and you take all the bows. This party dessert is an easy make-ahead.
Bake at 350° for 30 minutes. Makes 16 servings

1 package chocolate cake mix
2 eggs
  Water
1 quart strawberry ice cream, softened
1 quart pistachio ice cream, softened
2 envelopes (2 ounces each) whipped topping
  mix
  Milk
  Red food coloring
1 tablespoon light rum (optional)
  Chopped pistachio nuts

1 Grease two 9x1½-inch round layer-cake pans; dust with flour; tap out any excess.
2 Prepare cake mix with eggs and water, following label directions; pour into prepared pans.
3 Bake in moderate oven (350°) 30 minutes, or until centers spring back when lightly pressed with fingertip. Cool in pans on wire racks 10 minutes. Loosen layers around edges with a knife; turn out onto racks; cool completely. Split

1823

each layer, using a sawing motion with a sharp knife.

4 While layers bake, cut two 18-inch lengths of plastic wrap and fit into two 8-inch layer-cake pans.

5 Spread half the strawberry ice cream evenly in each cake pan. Top with half the pistachio ice cream in each pan. (Or use your favorite flavor combinations.) Cover ice cream with plastic wrap and freeze until ready to use.

6 Place one split cake layer on cookie sheet. Remove one ice-cream layer from pan; peel off transparent wrap and place on split layer; repeat with 2 more split layers and second ice-cream layer. (The extra split layer will make a nice treat for supper topped with a scoop of coffee ice cream.) Freeze entire cake while making frosting.

7 Beat whipped topping mix with milk, following label directions. Tint a pale pink with red food coloring and flavor with rum, if you wish.

8 Frost side and top of cake with part of frosting; pile remaining frosting onto center of cake and swirl out with teaspoon and sprinkle with pistachio nuts.

9 Freeze until frosting is firm; then cover with plastic wrap.

10 When ready to serve, loosen cake around edge of cookie sheet with a spatula dipped in hot water; transfer to serving plate with spatula and pancake turner. Cut with a sharp knife, or try your electric knife.

Sunshine Dessert Bowl
Makes 8 servings

1 packaged pound cake (9 ounces)
1 can (6 ounces) frozen concentrate for pineapple-orange juice, thawed
1 pint vanilla ice cream
⅓ cup light corn syrup
  Toasted slivered almonds

1 Cut pound cake into 8 thin slices crosswise and overlap in a small glass serving bowl. Drizzle with 6 tablespoons pineapple-orange concentrate. Chill.

2 Just before serving, stir corn syrup into remaining juice concentrate.

3 Scoop ice cream into center of serving bowl. Top with concentrate syrup and almonds.

Brazilian Log
Frost ice cream with whipped cream and top with chocolate—that's it!
Makes 6 servings

2 round pints vanilla ice cream
1 cup cream for whipping
2 tablespoons sugar
1 tablespoon instant coffee powder
1 square unsweetened chocolate

1 Remove ice cream from containers in one chunk by slitting cartons from top to bottom with a knife or scissors, then peel off. Place ice cream on a foil-lined cookie sheet to form a log; place in freezer while preparing cream.

2 Beat cream with sugar and instant coffee until stiff in a small bowl; spread over ice cream to cover completely.

3 Grate chocolate or shave into thin strips with a vegetable parer; sprinkle over top. Freeze until ready to serve. Cut in slices with a thin, sharp-blade knife.

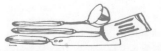

Royal Baked Alaska
Bake at 425° for 5 minutes. Makes 12 servings

1 package loaf-size yellow cake mix
½ gallon brick ice cream
4 egg whites
1 teaspoon vanilla
½ cup sugar

1 Prepare cake mix and bake in a greased cake pan, 9x9x2, following label directions.

2 When ready to put dessert together, place cake layer on 2 double-thick wide strips of foil crisscrossed on a cookie sheet. (This makes handling easier when dessert is hot from the oven.) Remove ice cream from carton and place on top of cake; trim cake to within ½ inch of ice cream. Freeze while making meringue.

3 Beat egg whites with vanilla until foamy-white and double in volume in a large bowl; sprinkle in sugar, a tablespoon at a time, beating all the time until sugar completely dissolves and meringue stands in firm peaks.

4 Spread over ice cream and cake, swirling in peaks, to cover completely. (Work quickly so ice cream doesn't melt.)

5 Bake in hot oven (425°) 5 minutes, or until peaks of meringue are toasty-golden. Slide onto a chilled serving plate; pull out foil strips. Cut dessert in slices with a thin, sharp-blade knife.

Raspberry Alaskas
Bake at 450° for 2 to 3 minutes. Makes 6 servings

1 pint vanilla ice cream
6 packaged dessert shells

3 egg whites
⅓ cup sugar
½ teaspoon vanilla
RASPBERRY SAUCE *(recipe follows)*

1 Scoop ice cream into 6 balls; place each in a dessert shell on a small cookie sheet; freeze several hours, or until firm.
2 Just before serving, beat egg whites until foamy-white and double in volume in a medium-size bowl; beat in sugar, 1 tablespoon at a time, until meringue stands in firm peaks; beat in vanilla. Spread over ice cream and cake shells to cover completely.
3 Bake in very hot oven (450°) 2 to 3 minutes, or until meringue is tipped with gold. Lift each onto a serving plate with a wide spatula. Serve at once with RASPBERRY SAUCE.

RASPBERRY SAUCE—Thaw 1 package (10 ounces) frozen red raspberries; drain syrup into a cup. Mix 1 tablespoon sugar and 2 teaspoons cornstarch in a small saucepan; stir in raspberry syrup. Cook, stirring constantly, until sauce thickens and boils 3 minutes; fold in raspberries; cool. Makes 1¼ cups.

Choffee Alaska
Easy to make and handsome! Ice-cream filling is chocolate and coffee molded in a bowl.
Bake cake base at 350° for 30 minutes, meringue at 450° for 2 to 3 minutes. Makes 8 servings

Ice-Cream Center
1½ pints chocolate ice cream
1½ pints coffee ice cream
Cake Base
4 tablespoons (½ stick) butter or margarine
¼ cup sugar
3 egg yolks
½ teaspoon vanilla
1½ tablespoons milk
½ cup sifted cake flour
½ teaspoon baking powder
⅛ teaspoon salt
Meringue
3 egg whites
¼ teaspoon cream of tartar
⅛ teaspoon salt
6 tablespoons sugar

1 Make ice-cream center: Line a 6-cup mixing bowl with slightly softened chocolate ice cream, shaping around edge to leave a hollow in middle; freeze until firm. Spoon coffee ice cream

into middle; smooth top flat with a knife. Freeze several hours, or overnight, or until very firm.
2 Make cake base: Cream butter or margarine with sugar until light and fluffy in medium-size bowl; beat in egg yolks, 1 at a time. (Egg whites make meringue in Step 7.)
3 Stir in vanilla and milk; sift in dry ingredients, blending well. Spread batter into a greased and floured 8x1½-inch layer-cake pan.
4 Bake in moderate oven (350°) 30 minutes, or until center springs back when lightly pressed with fingertip.
5 Cool in pan on wire rack 5 minutes; loosen around edge with knife; turn out onto rack; cool. (This much can be done a day ahead, ready for frosting and baking.)
6 When ready to serve, run a sharp-tip knife around top of ice-cream mold, then dip *very quickly* in and out of a pan of hot water. Unmold and set, round side up, onto cake layer; slide into freezer while preparing meringue.
7 Make meringue: Beat egg whites with cream of tartar and salt until foamy in medium-size bowl; beat in sugar, 1 tablespoon at a time, beating well after each addition, until meringue stands in firm peaks.
8 Set ice-cream-cake mold on 2 double-thick wide strips of foil crisscrossed on breadboard (for easy handling when mold is hot from the oven). Frost mold quickly with meringue, spreading meringue down to cover ice cream and cake completely. (Work fast so ice cream doesn't melt.)
9 Bake in very hot oven (450°) 2 to 3 minutes, or just until meringue peaks are lightly tipped with brown.
10 Slide mold onto a chilled serving plate; pull out foil strips; cut into wedge-shape pieces; serve at once.

Cantaloupe Alaska
This festive baked ice-cream dessert is much easier to make than you might think. If you have a freezer, divide ice cream into 6 mounds and freeze very firm before fixing cantaloupe and beating meringue.
Bake at 450° for 2 to 3 minutes. Makes 6 servings

4 egg whites
¼ teaspoon cream of tartar
¼ teaspoon salt
¼ cup sugar
1 ripe large cantaloupe
1 quart pistachio ice cream
Chopped pistachio nuts

1825

1 Place egg whites, cream of tartar, and salt in large bowl; beat until foamy; add sugar, 1 tablespoon at a time, beating after each addition until meringue forms stiff peaks.

2 Cut cantaloupe into 6 wedges; scoop out seeds; cut a thin slice from bottom of each wedge to make it stand steady; place on cookie sheet or breadboard; top each wedge with large scoop of very firm ice cream; cover completely with meringue, spreading it down to cantaloupe rind.

3 Bake in very hot oven (450°) 2 to 3 minutes, or until meringue is tipped with gold; sprinkle lightly with pistachio nuts; serve at once.

Rainbow Party Pie
Scoop sherbets into a ladyfinger crust and top with sparkly sauce.
Makes 6 to 8 servings

12 ladyfingers
¼ cup apricot preserves
1 pint lime sherbet
1 pint orange sherbet
1 pint lemon sherbet
    LEMON SPARKLE SAUCE (recipe follows)

1 Separate ladyfingers to make 24 pieces; spread flat side of each with preserves. Stand upright, rounded side out, ½ inch apart, around edge of a 9-inch pie plate; lay remaining in bottom.

2 Scoop sherbets into small balls; pile into prepared crust. Freeze at least four hours, or overnight.

3 When ready to serve, drizzle with part of the LEMON SPARKLE SAUCE; cut pie into wedges. Pass remaining sauce separately.

    LEMON SPARKLE SAUCE—Mix ½ cup sugar and 1 tablespoon cornstarch in a small saucepan; stir in 1 cup water. Cook, stirring constantly, until mixture thickens and boils 3 minutes; remove from heat. Stir in 3 tablespoons butter or margarine, 3 tablespoons lemon juice and ½ teaspoon grated lemon peel; cool. Makes about 1½ cups.

1826

Meringue Fantastique
Make the shell for this scrumptious dessert the day before or early the day of the party.
Bake at 275° for 1 hour. Makes 8 servings

1 eight-inch yellow- or white-cake layer
2 egg whites

¼ teaspoon salt
½ cup sugar
1 quart vanilla ice cream
    GOLDEN BUTTERSCOTCH SAUCE (recipe follows)
    Salted toasted almonds

1 Make cake from packaged mix or your own recipe.

2 Beat egg whites with salt until foamy in large bowl. Beat in sugar, 1 tablespoon at a time, until meringue stands in firm peaks.

3 Place cake layer on a sheet of brown paper on ungreased cookie sheet; frost top and side with meringue, building up side to make a 2-inch-high shell.

4 Bake in very slow oven (275°) 1 hour, or until dry; slide cake and shell from paper base with 2 spatulas; cool completely on wire rack.

5 Scoop ice cream into 8 balls (these can be made ahead of time and kept in freezer); fill meringue shell with ice cream; spoon GOLDEN BUTTERSCOTCH SAUCE over; sprinkle with almonds.

6 To serve, cut into wedges; pass any remaining sauce.

Golden Butterscotch Sauce
Makes about 1½ cups

2 cups firmly packed brown sugar
¼ cup dark corn syrup
3 tablespoons water
1 tablespoon lemon juice
¾ teaspoon salt
1 tablespoon butter or margarine
1 teaspoon vanilla

1 Mix sugar, corn syrup, water, lemon juice and salt in medium-size saucepan; heat slowly, stirring until sugar is dissolved; add butter or margarine.

2 Heat to boiling; cook, without stirring, until candy thermometer reads 230° (or until a fine thread spins from the end of a fork when dipped into hot syrup).

3 Remove from heat; stir in vanilla; cool.

Coffee Meringue Glacé
Crisp coffee meringue shell is filled with vanilla ice cream, topped with a mocha sauce.
Bake at 275° for 1½ to 2 hours. Makes 10 servings

4 egg whites
1 cup sugar

3 tablespoons instant coffee powder
⅛ teaspoon salt
1 quart vanilla ice cream
2 tablespoons finely chopped walnuts
  MOCHA SAUCE (recipe follows)

1 Beat egg whites until stiff but not dry. Mix sugar with coffee and salt; gradually beat into egg whites.
2 Cover cookie sheet with aluminum foil; mark off a 9-inch circle on foil. Spread meringue within circle, building up the edge to about 2 inches.
3 Bake in slow oven (275°) 1½ to 2 hours, or until crisp and dry. Remove from oven; cool. Carefully peel away foil; place meringue on serving plate.
4 Fill shell with ice cream; drizzle with the MOCHA SAUCE. Sprinkle with chopped walnuts. Cut in wedges to serve; spoon more sauce over each serving.

Mocha Sauce
Makes about 2 cups

1 package (6 ounces) semisweet-chocolate pieces (1 cup)
¼ cup (½ stick) butter or margarine
1 cup sifted 10X (confectioners' powdered) sugar
½ cup light corn syrup
2 teaspoons instant coffee powder
  Dash of salt
½ cup hot water
1 teaspoon vanilla

1 Melt chocolate pieces with butter or margarine in top of a double boiler over simmering water.
2 Stir in sugar, corn syrup, instant coffee, salt, hot water and vanilla until sauce is smooth and slightly thickened. Remove from heat. Serve at room temperature.

SAUCES FOR SUNDAES AND OTHER ICE CREAM DESSERTS

Hot Fudge Sauce
Makes about 1 cup

¾ cup light corn syrup
½ cup dry cocoa (not a mix)
  Dash of salt

⅓ cup butter or margarine
½ teaspoon vanilla

1 Combine syrup, cocoa and salt in a small saucepan. Heat slowly, stirring constantly, to boiling; simmer 3 minutes. Remove from heat.
2 Stir in butter or margarine and vanilla. Serve warm over ice cream or vanilla pudding.

Jiffy Fudge Sauce
Makes about 1 cup

1 cup semisweet-chocolate pieces
¾ cup light corn syrup
¼ cup milk
1 tablespoon butter or margarine
½ teaspoon vanilla

Place all ingredients in the top of a double boiler, set over simmering water and heat until smooth and creamy. Store in refrigerator.

Mint Fudge Sauce
Makes 1¼ cups

1 package (about 8¼ ounces) mint-flavor chocolate candy wafers
½ cup evaporated milk

Heat candy wafers and evaporated milk in the top of a double boiler, set over simmering water, stirring often, just until candy is melted and smooth. Serve warm or cold. Store in refrigerator.

Chocolate Truffle Sauce
Makes about 1 cup

1 package (6 ounces) semisweet-chocolate pieces
¾ cup eggnog (from a 4-cup container)

Melt semisweet-chocolate pieces in top of a double boiler over simmering water. Stir in eggnog until well blended. Serve warm or cold. Store in refrigerator.

Chocolate Velvet Sauce
Makes 1 cup

½ pound (32) marshmallows
2 squares (1 ounce each) unsweetened chocolate

1827

½ cup evaporated milk
1 teaspoon vanilla

Melt marshmallows and chocolate in the top of a double boiler over simmering water, stirring often, until creamy-smooth. Gradually blend in evaporated milk; stir in vanilla. Serve warm or cold. Store in refrigerator.

Chocolate Sundae Sauce
Makes 1 cup

1 package (6 ounces) semisweet-chocolate pieces
2 tablespoons butter or margarine
1 cup sifted 10X (confectioners' powdered) sugar
½ cup hot milk
1 teaspoon vanilla

1 Combine semisweet-chocolate pieces and butter or margarine in top of small double boiler; heat over simmering water, stirring often, 10 to 12 minutes, or until chocolate is melted.
2 Add 10X sugar alternately with hot milk; beat until smooth; stir in vanilla; serve warm or cold over your favorite ice cream.

Chocolate-Nut Sauce
Bits of not-quite-melted chocolate and walnuts give this sauce a pleasing crunch.
Makes about 1¼ cups

4 tablespoons (½ stick) butter or margarine
2 tablespoons light corn syrup
1 cup (6-ounce package) semisweet-chocolate pieces
1 cup chopped walnuts

1828

Melt butter or margarine in small heavy saucepan; remove from heat. Blend in corn syrup; stir in semisweet-chocolate pieces until almost melted, then walnuts. Serve warm.

Easy Mocha Sauce
Makes 1¼ cups

1 package chocolate-flavor instant-pudding mix
1 tablespoon instant coffee powder
1 cup light corn syrup
¼ cup warm water

Blend instant-pudding mix, instant coffee powder and corn syrup in a small bowl; stir in ¼ cup water just until smooth. Store in refrigerator.

Java Sauce
Makes about 1½ cups

2 tablespoons instant coffee powder
½ cup cream for whipping
1 cup light corn syrup

Place all ingredients in the top of a double boiler, set over simmering water and heat and stir until creamy-smooth. Serve warm or cold. Store in refrigerator.

Butterscotch Sauce
Makes 1 cup

1¼ cups firmly packed light brown sugar
½ cup light cream or table cream
2 tablespoons light corn syrup
4 tablespoons butter or margarine
1 teaspoon vanilla

Combine brown sugar, cream, corn syrup and butter or margarine in a small saucepan. Heat to boiling; boil 1 minute. Remove from heat and stir in vanilla. Serve warm or cold. Store in refrigerator.

Praline Sauce
Makes 1½ cups sauce

1 cup firmly packed dark brown sugar
½ cup light corn syrup
¼ cup (½ stick) butter or margarine
⅛ teaspoon salt
½ cup chopped pecans

1 Combine sugar, corn syrup, butter or margarine and salt in a medium-size saucepan. Cook over low heat, stirring constantly, until sugar dissolves. Bring to boiling; boil 2 minutes.
2 Remove from heat and mix in pecans. Serve warm.

Caramel-Walnut Sauce
Makes about 1½ cups

½ pound caramel-candy cubes
¾ cup water
½ cup chopped walnuts

Place caramels and water in the top of a double boiler, set over simmering water and heat and stir until smooth and creamy. Mix in nuts. Store in refrigerator.

Toffee-Walnut Sauce

Drizzle this super-rich creamy sauce over ice cream or squares of plain cake topped with whipped cream.
Makes 2 cups

¾ cup firmly packed light brown sugar
1 tablespoon instant coffee powder
 Dash of salt
½ cup water
1 can (about 15 ounces) sweetened condensed milk
½ cup chopped walnuts
1 teaspoon vanilla

1 Combine brown sugar, instant coffee, salt and water in a small heavy saucepan; heat, stirring constantly, to boiling, then cook, without stirring, to 230° on a candy thermometer. (A little syrup will spin fine threads when dropped from tip of spoon.) Remove from heat.
2 Blend hot syrup very slowly into sweetened condensed (*not evaporated*) milk in a medium-size bowl; stir in walnuts and vanilla. Serve warm or cold.

Butterscotch Sparkle Sauce

Makes about 1½ cups

2 cups firmly packed brown sugar
¼ cup dark corn syrup
3 tablespoons water
1 tablespoon lemon juice
¾ teaspoon salt
1 tablespoon butter or margarine
1 teaspoon vanilla

1 Mix sugar, corn syrup, water, lemon juice and salt in medium-size saucepan; heat slowly, stirring until sugar is dissolved; add butter or margarine.
2 Heat to boiling; cook, without stirring, until candy thermometer reads 230° (or until a fine thread spins from the end of a fork when dipped into hot syrup).
3 Remove from heat; stir in vanilla; cool.

Sparkle Ice-Cream Sauce

It goes together with no fussy syrup cooking and keeps its sparkle to the last drop.
Makes 4 cups

2 cups firmly packed light brown sugar
1 cup water
2 cups (1-pint bottle) light corn syrup
½ teaspoon salt

Combine brown sugar and water in a medium-size saucepan. Heat to boiling, stirring until brown sugar dissolves, then cook 5 minutes; remove from heat. Stir in corn syrup and salt; cool.

Creamy Rum Sauce

Makes 3 cups

1 egg
¼ cup sugar
 Dash of salt
4 tablespoons (½ stick) butter or margarine
½ teaspoon rum flavoring extract
1 cup cream for whipping

1 Heat egg in the top of a small double boiler over simmering water, beating all the time and adding sugar gradually until mixture is creamy-thick; stir in salt. (Beating will take about two minutes.)
2 Beat in butter or margarine, a thin slice at a time, keeping top over simmering water and beating constantly, until creamy again. Pour into a bowl; stir in rum flavoring; Chill until ready to serve.
3 Beat cream until stiff in a medium-size bowl; spoon on top of chilled mixture and fold in. (Tip: Use a portable electric mixer for beating and plan to use the sauce up the first time around—it tends to lose its fluffiness upon standing.)

VARIATIONS:

Fluffy Vanilla Sauce: Prepare as directed for CREAMY RUM SAUCE but substitute 1 teaspoon vanilla for the rum flavoring extract.
Fluffy Wine Sauce: Prepare as directed for CREAMY RUM SAUCE but substitute 1 tablespoon cream sherry, ruby port or sweet Madeira wine for the rum flavoring extract.

Marshmallow Sauce

Makes about 1½ cups

½ cup light corn syrup
½ cup light cream or table cream
1 cup tiny marshmallows
½ teaspoon vanilla

1829

Place corn syrup, cream and marshmallows in the top of a double boiler, set over simmering water and heat and stir until creamy-smooth. Remove from heat, stir in vanilla. Serve warm or cold. Store in refrigerator.

Maple Fluff Sauce
Makes about 1½ cups

1 cup blended maple syrup
1 cup tiny marshmallows

Place all ingredients in the top of a double boiler, set over simmering water and heat and stir until creamy-smooth. Serve warm or cold. Store in refrigerator.

Pink Peppermint Sauce
Makes about 1¼ cups

1 cup bottled marshmallow topping
¼ cup light corn syrup
½ cup crushed pink peppermint candies
   Few drops red food coloring

Place all ingredients in the top of a double boiler, set over simmering water and heat and stir until creamy-smooth. Serve warm or cold. Store in refrigerator.

Golden Fruit Sauce
Makes about 2 cups

1 can (about 1 pound) fruit cocktail
1 tablespoon cornstarch
2 tablespoons lemon juice
1½ teaspoons grated lemon peel

1 Drain syrup from fruit cocktail into a cup. Set fruit aside for Step 3.
2 Blend cornstarch into a few tablespoons of the syrup until smooth in a small saucepan, then stir in remaining syrup and lemon juice.
3 Cook, stirring constantly, over medium heat, until sauce thickens and boils 3 minutes; stir in fruit and lemon peel. Serve warm.

1830

Currant Sparkle Sauce
Makes 1¼ cups

1 cup currant jelly
¼ cup water
2 teaspoons lemon juice

Place currant jelly and water in a small saucepan and cook over low heat, stirring constantly, until jelly is melted and mixture smooth. Remove from heat and stir in lemon juice. Cool before serving.

SOME JIFFY TOPPINGS FOR ICE CREAM DESSERTS

1 Frozen concentrated orange, tangerine or grape juice, thawed slightly.
2 Baby-food peaches, plums, apples or apricots.
3 Thick amber molasses.
4 Melted jelly or orange marmalade.
5 Frozen strawberries, raspberries, peaches, mixed fruits, slightly thawed.
6 Crushed peanut, pecan or almond brittle.
7 Crushed peppermint candy.
8 Grated chocolate or chocolate curls.
9 Instant-cocoa mix.
10 Creamy topping or whipped cream in a pressurized can.

ICE CREAM SODAS, MILK SHAKES, FROSTS AND OTHER SODA FOUNTAIN DRINKS

Basic Chocolate Soda
Makes 4 servings

½ cup canned chocolate-flavor syrup
4 tablespoons cream for whipping
1 pint vanilla ice cream
2 bottles (7 ounces each) carbonated water, chilled

1 Measure 2 tablespoons of the chocolate-flavor syrup, then 1 tablespoon cream into each of 4 tall glasses.
2 Add a small scoop of ice cream to each glass and mash lightly into chocolate-flavor syrup and cream.
3 Add enough carbonated water to each glass to half-fill. Drop a large scoop of ice cream into each glass and add more carbonated water to fill glasses.

VARIATIONS:

Double Chocolate Soda—Prepare as directed for BASIC CHOCOLATE SODA but substitute chocolate ice cream for vanilla.

Chocolate Mint Soda—Prepare as directed for BASIC CHOCOLATE SODA but add a drop of peppermint extract to each glass along with chocolate syrup and substitute peppermint ice cream for vanilla.

Mocha Ice-Cream Soda—Prepare as directed for BASIC CHOCOLATE SODA but substitute coffee ice cream for vanilla.

Coffee-Cola Soda
Makes 4 servings

¼ cup chocolate-flavor syrup
4 tablespoons light cream or table cream
1 pint coffee ice cream
2 or 3 bottles cola beverage, chilled

1 Measure 1 tablespoon of the chocolate-flavor syrup, then 1 tablespoon light cream or table cream into each of 4 tall glasses.
2 Add a small scoop of ice cream to each glass and mash lightly into chocolate-flavor syrup and cream.
3 Add enough cola beverage to each glass to half fill. Drop a large scoop of ice cream into each glass and add more cola beverage to fill glasses.

Coffee Ice-Cream Soda
Makes 4 sodas

4 teaspoons instant coffee powder
4 teaspoons sugar
½ cup light cream or table cream
2 bottles (7 ounces each) carbonated water, chilled
1 pint vanilla ice cream

1 Stir instant coffee and sugar into cream in measuring cup; divide among 4 tall glasses.
2 Pour in carbonated water to fill each glass ⅔ full.
3 Top each with a spoonful of ice cream and more carbonated water.

Strawberry Ice-Cream Soda
Makes 4 servings

1 package (10 ounces) frozen sliced strawberries
4 tablespoons bottled strawberry syrup or melba sauce (optional)
1 pint strawberry ice cream
2 bottles (7 ounces each) carbonated water, chilled

1 Place frozen sliced strawberries and, if you like, bottled strawberry syrup or melba sauce in an electric cup; beat at low speed about 30 seconds; stir with a rubber spatula, then beat at high speed about 1 minute until the consistency of sherbet.
2 Divide strawberry purée among 4 tall glasses. Add a small scoop of ice cream to each and mash into strawberry purée.
3 Add enough carbonated water to each glass to half fill. Drop a large scoop of ice cream into each glass and add more carbonated water to fill glasses.

VARIATIONS:

Raspberry Ice-Cream Soda—Prepare as directed for STRAWBERRY ICE-CREAM SODA but substitute 1 package (10 ounces) frozen raspberries for the strawberries and strain after puréeing. Also substitute raspberry ice cream for the strawberry.
Peach Ice-Cream Soda—Prepare as directed for STRAWBERRY ICE-CREAM SODA but substitute 1 package (10 ounces) frozen sliced peaches for the strawberries and omit the bottled strawberry syrup or melba sauce. Also substitute peach ice cream for the strawberry.

Orange Ice-Cream Soda
Makes 4 servings

4 teaspoons frozen concentrated orange juice
4 tablespoons light cream or table cream
1 pint orange sherbet
2 bottles (7 ounces each) carbonated water, chilled

1 Place 1 teaspoon frozen concentrated orange juice and 1 tablespoon light cream or table cream into each of 4 tall glasses.
2 Add a small scoop of orange sherbet to each glass and mash into orange concentrate mixture.
3 Add enough carbonated water to each glass to half fill. Drop in a large scoop of orange sherbet into each glass and add more carbonated water to fill glasses.

1831

SODA FOUNTAIN SENSATIONS

VARIATIONS:

Ginger-Orange Ice-Cream Soda—Prepare ORANGE ICE-CREAM SODA as directed but substitute ginger ale for carbonated water.
Citrus Soda—Prepare ORANGE ICE-CREAM SODA as directed but substitute lemon sherbet for the orange and lemon-flavor carbonated beverage for the carbonated water.
Sunburst Soda—Prepare ORANGE ICE-CREAM SODA as directed but substitute orange-flavor carbonated beverage for carbonated water and strawberry ice cream or raspberry sherbet for the orange sherbet.

Chocolate-Orange Fizz
Make 6 servings

12 tablespoons instant cocoa mix
1½ cups milk
1 pint orange sherbet
1 bottle (28 ounces) orange-flavor carbonated beverage, chilled

1 Measure 2 tablespoons of the cocoa mix and ¼ cup of the milk into each of 6 tall glasses; stir with cocoa mix dissolves.
2 Add a scoop or spoonful of orange sherbet to each glass; fill slowly with orange beverage. Garnish each with an orange slice, if you wish.

Black Cherry Bounce
Makes 4 servings

8 tablespoons bottled raspberry syrup
8 tablespoons light cream or table cream
1 bottle (28 ounces) black-cherry–flavor carbonated beverage
1 pint vanilla ice cream

1 Measure 2 tablespoons of the raspberry syrup, then 2 tablespoons cream into each of 4 tall glacses; pour in just enough of the black-cherry beverage to half-fill each glass.
2 Add 2 generous spoonfuls of ice cream to each; pour in remaining black-cherry beverage.

1832

Vermont Soda
Maple-rich through and through—and so easy children can be their own soda chefs.
Makes 2 servings

½ cup maple-blended syrup
1 cup milk

2 bottles (7 ounces each) carbonated water, chilled
½ pint maple-walnut ice cream
Walnut halves
Maraschino cherries

1 Pour syrup into 2 tall glasses; stir in milk and carbonated water. Top each with two small scoops of ice cream.
2 Garnish with walnut halves and maraschino cherries threaded onto kebab sticks.

Vanilla Milk Shake
Makes 4 servings

2¼ cups milk
½ pint vanilla ice cream
2 teaspoons vanilla

Combine all ingredients in an electric-blender container; cover; beat until creamy smooth. (Or combine all ingredients in a bowl and beat with an electric beater). Pour into tall glasses.

Maple-Pecan Milk Shake
Makes 4 servings

¼ cup maple-blended syrup
2 cups skim milk
½ pint (1 cup) butter-pecan ice cream

Combine all ingredients in an electric-blender container; cover; beat until creamy-smooth. (Or combine all ingredients in a bowl and beat with an electric beater. Pour into tall glasses.

APRICOT-BANANA ROYALE—Peel 1 medium-size ripe banana and slice; place in an electric-blender container. Add 2 tablespoons sugar, 2 cups milk, ½ cup bottled apricot-sour cocktail mix and ½ pint (1 cup) vanilla ice milk; cover. Beat until creamy-smooth. (Or mash banana in a bowl, then beat in remaining ingredients with an electric beater.) Makes 4 servings.
Note: If your blender container holds less than 4½ cups, prepare half of mixture at a time.

Chocolate Milk Shake
A shake you can make just that fast—thick with ice cream, of course.
Makes 6 servings

4 cups milk
¼ cup chocolate-flavor syrup (from an 11-ounce jar)
1 teaspoon vanilla
1 pint vanilla ice cream
6 marshmallows
6 peppermint sticks

1 Combine half each of the milk, chocolate syrup, vanilla and ice cream in an electric-blender container; cover. Beat until thick and smooth. Pour into glasses. Repeat with remaining half of ingredients. (If you do not have a blender, mix milk, syrup and vanilla in a large bowl, then beat in ice cream, a few spoonfuls at a time, with a rotary beater.)
2 Thread a marshmallow onto each peppermint stick; place one in each cup for a stirrer.

Chocolate-Peppermint Shake
Makes 4 servings

½ cup chocolate syrup
OR: ½ cup sweetened chocolate-flavored drink mix
½ cup marshmallow crème
3½ cups milk
¼ teaspoon peppermint extract

Combine chocolate syrup, marshmallow crème, milk and extract in electric-blender container; whirl at high speed 1 minute or until well mixed. Pour into tall glasses.

Candy-Stick Float
Doubly good with chocolate and peppermint—one of the most popular flavor combinations.
Makes 2 servings

½ pint vanilla ice cream
1½ cups milk
3 tablespoons chocolate-flavor syrup
¼ teaspoon peppermint extract
Peppermint ice cream
Peppermint-candy canes or sticks

1 Beat vanilla ice cream, milk, chocolate syrup and peppermint extract until foamy-thick in an electric blender or 4-cup measure; pour into 2 tall glasses.
2 Top each with a small scoop of peppermint ice cream. Garnish with a candy cane or peppermint-stick stirrer.

Maple syrup is the flavor secret of Vermont Soda.

Chocolate-Cherry Cooler
Makes 4 servings

1833

2 cups chocolate milk
1 pint (2 cups) cherry ice cream
1 teaspoon rum flavoring or extract

Combine all ingredients in an electric-blender container; cover; beat until creamy-smooth. (Or combine all ingredients in a bowl and beat with an electric beater.) Pour into tall glasses.
ORANGE-PINEAPPLE WHIRL—Thaw 1 can (6 ounces) frozen concentrate for orange-pineapple juice; place in an electric-blender container. Add 2 cups milk, ½ pint (1 cup) pineapple ice cream, and ¼ cup light corn syrup; cover. Beat until creamy-smooth. (Or combine all ingre-

dients in a bowl and beat with an electric beater.) Makes 4 servings.
Note: If your blender container holds less than 4½ cups, prepare half of each mixture at a time.

Super Mocha Milk Shake
Makes 4 servings

1 pint block vanilla and chocolate ice cream
2 tablespoons sugar
2 tablespoons coffee-flavor instant cereal beverage
3 cups milk

Combine half the ingredients at a time in an electric blender; mix at high speed for 1 minute. (Or beat in a bowl with a rotary beater.) Serve in tall glasses.

Choco-Banana Flip
Makes 6 servings

¾ cup instant nonfat dry milk
3 cups ice water
1 can (about 5 ounces) chocolate flavor syrup
2 medium-size ripe bananas
½ pint vanilla ice cream

1 Combine dry milk and ice water in an electric-blender container; cover. Beat until smooth. Add chocolate syrup; beat until blended.
2 Peel bananas and slice; add to chocolate mixture with ice cream; beat until smooth. Pour into tall glasses. (If you do not have a blender, mash bananas well; combine with other ingredients in a bowl and beat with an electric beater until well blended.)

Rio Cream
Pouf of cinnamon cream crowns each thick coffee-flavor shake.
Makes 4 servings

1 pint coffee ice cream
1½ cups milk
⅛ teaspoon ground cinnamon
½ cup cream for whipping
1 tablespoon cinnamon-sugar
  Cinnamon sticks

1 Beat ice cream, milk and cinnamon until foamy-thick in an electric blender or 4-cup measure; pour into 4 large glasses.

2 Beat cream with cinnamon-sugar until stiff in a small bowl; float a spoonful on top of each glass. Garnish each with a cinnamon-stick stirrer.

Double Strawberry Dream
Makes 6 servings

1 package (10 ounces) frozen sliced strawberries, partly thawed
½ pint strawberry ice cream
1 large ripe banana, peeled and cut up
2 cups milk
1 teaspoon vanilla

1 Combine strawberries, ice cream, banana, 1 cup of the milk and vanilla in an electric-blender container; cover. Beat until creamy-smooth. Stir in remaining 1 cup milk.
2 Pour into 6 tall glasses. Garnish each with several fresh strawberries threaded onto a kebab stick, if you wish.
Note: If you do not have a blender, beat strawberries with ice cream and banana in large bowl of electric mixer, then stir in milk and vanilla.

Strawberry Smoothie
Makes 8 servings

1 package (10 ounces) frozen sliced strawberries, thawed
4 cups milk
1 pint strawberry ice cream
1 teaspoon grated lemon peel

Combine half the ingredients at a time in an electric blender; mix at high speed for 1 minute. (Or beat in a bowl with a rotary beater.) Serve in tall glasses.

Tutti-Frutti Blush
Makes 4 servings

1 can (about 8 ounces) fruit cocktail
½ cup bottled grenadine syrup
1 pint (2 cups) strawberry ice cream
2 cups milk

Combine all ingredients in an electric-blender container; cover; beat until creamy-smooth. (Or combine all ingredients in a bowl and beat with an electric beater. Pour into tall glasses.

PEACH FROSTY—Place 1 can (8 ounces) cling-peach slices and syrup in an electric-blender container. Add 2 cups milk, ¾ pint (1½ cups) vanilla ice cream and ¼ teaspoon almond extract; cover. Beat until creamy-smooth. (Or beat peaches until smooth in a bowl with an electric beater; slowly beat in remaining ingredients.) Makes 4 servings.

Orange-Vanilla Freeze
Makes 4 servings

1 can (6 ounces) frozen orange-juice concentrate, partially thawed
2½ cups milk
1 pint vanilla ice cream, softened
¼ teaspoon ground cinnamon

Combine orange-juice concentrate, milk ice cream and cinnamon in electric-blender container; whirl at high speed about 1 minute, or until well mixed. Pour into tall glasses or mugs.

Peach Dream
Makes 4 servings

1 can (about 1 pound) cling peach slices, drained and cut up
1 pint vanilla ice cream
¼ cup orange juice
½ teaspoon vanilla
¼ teaspoon almond extract
1½ cups milk
Red food coloring
ORANGE CROWNS (directions follow)

1 Beat peaches, ice cream, orange juice, vanilla and almond extract until smooth in an electric blender; stir in milk and a drop of red food coloring. (If you do not have a blender, chop peaches fine, then combine with remaining ingredients in a medium-size bowl and beat with an electric beater.)
2 Pour into 4 tall glasses; slip an ORANGE CROWN, pointed end up, over each glass.

ORANGE CROWNS—Cut 4 slices, ⅛ inch thick, from a large seedless orange. Carefully separate the wedges of each, leaving them attached to rind.

Apricot Frost
Makes 4 servings

1 pint vanilla ice cream
2 cups milk
¼ cup apricot preserves (from a 12-ounce jar)
4 sprigs mint

1 Beat half of the ice cream, milk and apricot preserves until foamy-thick in an electric blender or 4-cup measure; pour into 4 tall glasses.
2 Spoon remaining ice cream, dividing evenly, on top. Garnish each with a sprig of mint.

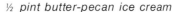

Peanut Whizz
Especially for youngsters—and you can whizz it up in a jiffy in your blender.
Makes 2 servings

½ pint butter-pecan ice cream
1½ cups milk
4 tablespoons peanut butter
2 tablespoons honey
Chopped peanuts

Beat ice cream, milk, peanut butter and honey until foamy-thick in an electric blender or 4-cup measure; pour into 2 tall glasses. Sprinkle with chopped peanuts.

SOUP KETTLE:
BASIC SOUP STOCKS, CLEAR AND THIN SOUPS, BISQUES AND CREAM SOUPS, VEGETABLE SOUPS, HEARTY SOUPS AND CHOWDERS, DESSERT SOUPS, OUT-OF-THE CAN QUICKIES

Soup! The very name conjures up visions of giant kettles simmering lazily on the back of the stove. And memories of broth and onions and carrots and celery sending their heady aroma throughout the house. Comforting memories, these, because there is something particularly warming about a bowl of soup, be it thick or thin, hot or cold, light or heavy, homemade, canned or even one of the new instant varieties.

Soups can be served at almost any course of the meal. As appetizers, of course—light, fragrant soups that set the stage for the food to follow. They can be the star attraction, the meal itself, if they are meaty enough. They can even be served as dessert—in Europe, fruit soups are commonly served as the finale to a fine dinner.

This section of soups is a big one, including all categories of soups, all flavors. There are soups that begin with a soupbone and those that begin with a box. There are soups that take hours to make and others that require only seconds. There are summer soups and winter soups, family soups and party soups. In short, soups for every taste and every occasion.

BASIC SOUP STOCKS

1837

Basic Beef Stock
Make this flavorful beef broth that is the basic stock for a variety of soups to follow.
Makes 14 cups

2½ pounds brisket, boneless chuck or bottom round, in one piece
2 pounds shin of beef with bones
2 three-inch marrow bones
1 veal knuckle (about 1 pound)
Water
8 teaspoons salt

Oyster Chowder begins with canned oyster stew, adds canned lobster, potatoes, whole-kernel corn and peas.

SOUP KETTLE

2 carrots, pared
2 medium-size yellow onions, peeled
2 stalks celery with leaves
1 turnip, pared and quartered
1 leek, washed well
3 large sprigs of parsley
12 peppercorns
3 whole cloves
1 bay leaf

1 Place beef, shin of beef, marrow bones and veal knuckle in a large kettle; add water to cover, about 4 quarts. Heat to boiling; skim off foam that appears on top. Add salt, carrots, onions, celery, turnip and leek; tie parsley, peppercorns, cloves and bay leaf in a small cheesecloth bag; add to kettle. Push under the liquid and add more water if needed.
2 Heat to boiling; cover; reduce heat; simmer very slowly 3½ to 4 hours, or until meat is tender. Remove meat and vegetables from broth.
3 Strain broth through cheesecloth into a large bowl. (There should be about 14 cups.) Use this stock in any recipe calling for beef broth.
4 When meat is cool enough to handle, remove and discard bones. Trim large piece of meat and save for a main-dish recipe, if you wish. Cut trimmings and shin beef into bite-size pieces; use as called for in following recipes. To store in refrigerator up to 3 to 4 days, keep in covered container. To freeze, pack in small portions, 1 or 2 cups, in plastic bags or freezer containers, to use as needed.
5 To store in refrigerator, up to 4 days, leave fat layer on surface of broth until ready to use, then lift off and discard before heating. To freeze: Transfer broth to freezer containers, allowing space on top for expansion; freeze until ready to use (3 to 4 months maximum).

Basic Chicken Stock

It is well worthwhile to make homemade chicken broth. This recipe gives you enough broth and meat to make 2 soups and even extra meat for a salad or casserole, if you wish.
Makes 12 cups

2 broiler-fryers, 3 to 3½ pounds each
    Chicken giblets
2 medium carrots, pared
1 large parsnip, pared
1 large onion, chopped (1 cup)
2 stalks celery
2 celery tops
3 sprigs parsley

1 leek, washed well
Water
2 tablespoons salt
12 peppercorns

1 Combine chicken, chicken giblets, carrots, parsnip, onion and celery in a large kettle; tie celery tops, parsley and leek together with a string; add to kettle. Add enough cold water to cover chicken and vegetables, about 12 cups.
2 Heat slowly to boiling; skim; add salt and peppercorns; reduce heat. Simmer very slowly 1 to 1½ hours, or until meat falls off the bones. Remove meat and vegetables, discard the bundle of greens.
3 Strain broth through cheesecloth into a large bowl. (There should be about 12 cups.) Use this delicious stock in any recipe calling for chicken broth.
4 When cool enough to handle, remove and discard skin and bones from chicken; cut meat into bite-size pieces; use as called for in following recipes, or use in salads, casseroles, etc. To store in refrigerator, up to 3 to 4 days, keep in covered container. To freeze, pack in small portions, 1 or 2 cups, in plastic bags or freezer containers, to use as needed.
5 To store in refrigerator, up to 4 days, leave fat layer on surface of broth until ready to use, then lift fat off and discard, or use in other cooking. To freeze, transfer broth to freezer containers, allowing space on top for expansion. Freeze until ready to use (3 to 4 months maximum).

Basic Vegetable Stock
Makes about 6 cups

4 cups water
2 cups chopped celery stalks and leaves
1 large onion, chopped
½ cup chopped cabbage
1 carrot diced
6 peppercorns
1½ teaspoons salt
1 bay leaf
¼ teaspoon monosodium glutamate
2½ cups (1 No. 2 can) tomato juice

Combine all ingredients in a 3-quart saucepan; simmer covered about 1 hour; strain. Serve hot as vegetable bouillon, or use as a stock for making soup.

CLEAR SOUPS AND THIN SOUPS

Tomato Consommé
Makes 8 servings

2 cups water
4 beef-bouillon cubes
  Handful of celery leaves
1 medium-size onion, peeled and sliced
¼ cup chopped parsley
1 teaspoon salt
½ teaspoon leaf basil, crumbled
2 bay leaves
1 can (46 ounces) tomato juice

1 Combine water, bouillon cubes, celery leaves, onion, parsley, salt, basil and bay leaves in a large saucepan; heat to boiling, then simmer 15 minutes.
2 Stir in tomato juice; heat 5 minutes longer, or until bubbly-hot. Strain into heated soup bowls or cups.

Hot Spiced Tomato Cup
Serve this tangy dinner starter in dainty cups with a crisp nibble.
Makes 12 servings

2 bottles (1 pint, 10 ounces each) tomato-juice
  cocktail
½ teaspoon ground allspice
1 lemon, cut in 12 thin slices

1 Mix tomato-juice cocktail and allspice in a large saucepan; heat, stirring several times, to boiling.
2 Pour into small cups; float a slice of lemon on each. Serve hot.

Bouillon Imperial
Makes 6 servings

2 cans (10½ ounces each) condensed beef
  broth
1 cup water
½ cup thinly sliced celery
½ cup thinly sliced radishes

1 Combine beef broth, water and celery in a medium-size saucepan; heat to boiling; cover. Simmer 10 minutes, or just until celery is crisply tender.
2 Ladle into soup bowls or cups; float radish slices on top. Serve with crisp thin wheat crackers, if you wish.

Tomato Consommé, a colorful, tasty party-starter.

SOUP KETTLE

Harvest Bouillon
Makes 8 servings

        2 cans (10½ ounces each) condensed beef
          broth
     ⅔ cup apple cider
     ⅔ cup water
        2 tablespoons lemon juice
        8 paper-thin slices of lemon
          Parsley

1 Combine bouillon, apple cider, water and lemon juice in pitcher; chill.
2 At serving time, pour into glasses or punch cups and garnish with lemon slices and parsley.

Sherried Mushroom Bouillon
Makes 4 servings

        1 can (3 or 4 ounces) sliced mushrooms
        3 green onions, trimmed and sliced thin
        1 tablespoon lemon juice
        1 can (10½ ounces) condensed beef broth
     1⅓ cups water
        1 tablespoon dry sherry

1 Combine mushrooms and liquid, green onions and lemon juice in a medium-size saucepan. Heat to boiling; cover. Simmer 3 minutes.
2 Stir in beef broth and water. Heat to boiling. Turn off heat, stir in sherry.
3 Pour into soup cups; sprinkle with chopped parsley, if you wish.

Herbed Chicken Consommé
Makes 8 servings

        3 cans (about 14 ounces each) chicken broth
        1 teaspoon leaf tarragon, crumbled
     ½ teaspoon leaf thyme, crumbled
        1 small lemon, sliced
        1 small onion, peeled and sliced
        4 peppercorns
        2 envelopes unflavored gelatin
        2 cups (16-ounce carton) dairy sour cream

1 Pour broth into a large saucepan; skim off fat, if any.
2 Stir tarragon, thyme, lemon, onion and peppercorns into broth; sprinkle gelatin over top; let stand several minutes to soften gelatin.
3 Heat slowly to boiling; simmer 5 minutes; strain into a large shallow pan. Cool, then chill at least 2 hours, or until firm.
4 Just before serving, cut gelatin into tiny cubes; spoon cubes, alternately with sour cream, into parfait glasses. Garnish each with a sprig of parsley, if you wish.

Clear Turkey Noodle Soup
It's rich with homemade noodles—a real farm-style main-dish-of-the-meal.
Makes 8 generous servings

     12 cups TURKEY BROTH (recipe follows)
        2 cups diced celery
        1 small onion, chopped (¼ cup)
        1 teaspoon salt
     ¼ teaspoon pepper
        1 recipe HOMEMADE EGG NOODLES (recipe follows)
          OR: 1 package (1 pound) wide egg noodles
     ¼ cup chopped parsley

1 Heat TURKEY BROTH, celery, onion, salt and pepper to boiling in large kettle. Drop in noodles, a few at a time, so broth does not stop boiling. Cook, stirring often, 10 minutes, or just until noodles are tender.
2 Stir in parsley; ladle into soup plates or big bowls.

Turkey Broth
Makes about 12 cups

Break turkey carcass enough to fit into a large kettle; add 1 sliced onion, 1 sliced carrot, handful of celery tops, 1 tablespoon salt, ¼ teaspoon pepper and water almost to cover (about 12 cups). Cover kettle; heat to boiling, then simmer 1 hour. Lift out carcass and, when cool enough to handle, remove any bits of meat and chop coarsely. Strain broth; add meat; cool, then chill enough to skim fat from top. If you plan to use it within a few days, store in covered jars in refrigerator; if to be used later, freeze in freezer containers.

Homemade Egg Noodles
If you have never made them, do try this easy recipe. Dough needs to dry, so mix it about 2 hours before cooking time.
Makes about 1 pound uncooked noodles

        4 eggs
        1 teaspoon salt
     2½ cups sifted all-purpose flour

1 Beat eggs well with salt in medium-size bowl. Stir in 1 cup flour, then mix in enough of remaining 1½ cups to make a stiff dough. (It should be slightly stiffer than piecrust dough.)
2 Turn out on floured pastry cloth or board; knead a few times to make dough smooth. Shape into a ball; cover with a clean tea towel; let rest on pastry cloth or board about 30 minutes.
3 Roll out half the dough into a large thin sheet; carefully roll sheet around rolling pin, then unroll and hang dough on tea towel spread on a rod or over back of straight-back chair (a broom handle set on the backs of 2 chairs makes a good rod). Repeat with remaining dough; let dough hang 30 minutes, or until dry but still pliable.
4 Roll up each sheet, jelly-roll fashion. Cut into ½-inch slices. Separate and unroll strips. Spread out on board to let dry, turning occasionally, about 30 minutes. Noodles are now ready to be cooked.

Chinese Egg-Drop Soup
Makes 6 servings

2 cans (14 ounces each) chicken broth
1 egg, slightly beaten
2 tablespoons chopped parsley

1 Heat chicken broth just to boiling in a medium-size saucepan. Pour in beaten egg very slowly, stirring constantly, just until egg cooks and separates into shreds.
2 Ladle into heated cups; sprinkle with parsley.

Greek Lemon Soup
Makes 6 to 8 servings

2 cans (10½ ounces each) condensed chicken broth
2 soup cans of water
⅓ cup uncooked regular rice
4 eggs
2 tablespoons lemon juice

1 Combine chicken broth and water in a large saucepan; heat to boiling. Stir in rice; cover. Cook 20 minutes, or until rice is tender; remove from heat.
2 Beat eggs until frothy-light in a medium-size bowl; slowly beat in lemon juice, then 1 cup

of the hot broth mixture; beat back into remaining broth mixture in saucepan. Heat slowly, stirring several times, just until hot. (Do not boil.)
3 Ladle into heated soup bowls or cups; sprinkle with parsley, if you wish.

Old-Time Lemon Soup
It's cool and tangy, with the fresh spark only lemon can add.
Makes 4 to 6 servings

1 envelope chicken-noodle–soup mix
1 cup thinly sliced celery
4 teaspoons lemon juice
2 hard-cooked eggs, finely diced

1 Prepare soup mix, following label directions; cook 5 minutes; add celery and cook 2 minutes longer.
2 Remove from heat; stir in lemon juice; pour into bowl; cover; chill.
3 Serve in cups or small bowls, with diced hard-cooked eggs to be sprinkled over.

Jellied Bouillon Julienne
Makes 6 servings

2 cans (10½ ounces each) condensed beef consommé, chilled
1 small stalk celery
½ small carrot, pared
6 radishes, washed and trimmed
½ small cucumber, pared
1 green onion, trimmed

1 Empty jellied consommé into a medium-size bowl; keep in refrigerator while cutting up vegetables.
2 Cut celery, carrot, radishes and cucumber into 1-inch-long strips; slice green onion thin; fold into consommé.
3 Chill, stirring once or twice, at least 1 hour before serving.

Jellied Lemon Strata
Makes 4 servings

1 envelope unflavored gelatin
1 can (about 14 ounces) chicken broth
1 teaspoon grated lemon peel
2 tablespoons lemon juice
¼ teaspoon salt

1841

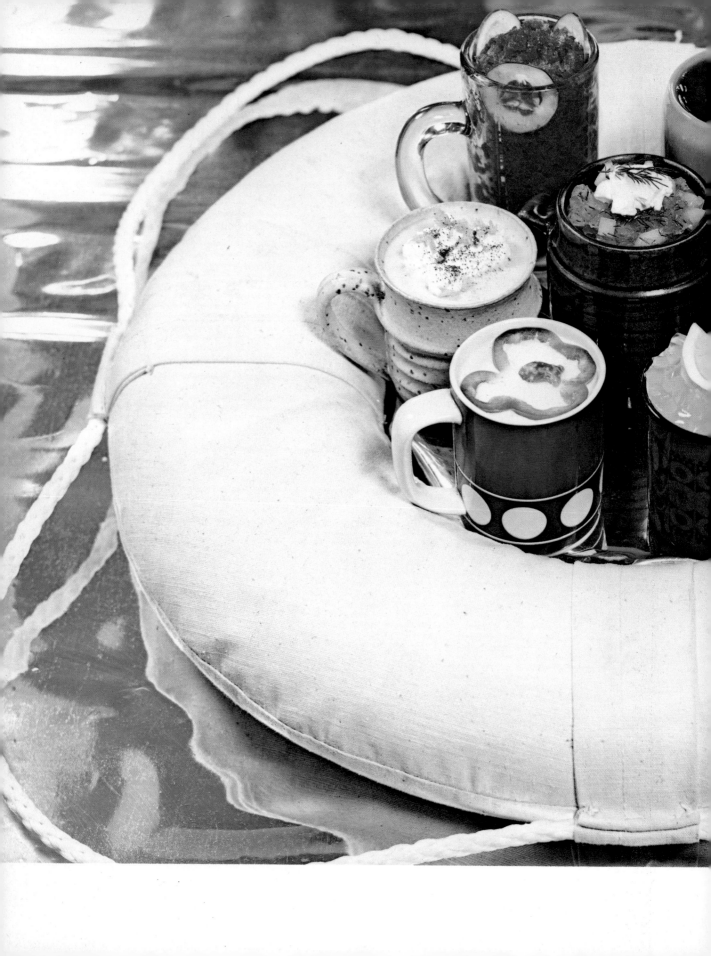

2 hard-cooked eggs, shelled
2 tablespoons chopped parsley

1 Soften gelatin in 1 cup of the chicken broth in a small saucepan; heat, stirring constantly, until gelatin dissolves; remove from heat.
2 Stir in remaining chicken broth, lemon peel and juice and salt; pour into a baking dish, 9x9x2. Chill several hours.
3 Chop eggs coarsely; toss with parsley in a small bowl.
4 Cut gelatin mixture lengthwise and crosswise into ¼-inch cubes; spoon half into tall cups or parfait glasses. Top with egg mixture, then remaining gelatin mixture. Garnish each serving with a sprig of parsley, if you wish.

●

Quick Jellied Borsch
Makes 6 servings

1 envelope unflavored gelatin
1½ cups cold water
1 tablespoon instant beef bouillon
    OR: 3 beef-bouillon cubes
1 can (about 1 pound) diced beets
4 teaspoons prepared horseradish
1 tablespoon lemon juice
    Dairy sour cream
    Celery seeds

1 Soften gelatin in ½ cup cold water in medium-size saucepan; stir in remaining 1 cup water and instant beef bouillon or cubes; heat, stirring constantly, just until gelatin and bouillon are dissolved.
2 Combine beets and juice, horseradish and lemon juice in medium-size bowl; stir in hot gelatin mixture; chill until thickened (it will not be firm).
3 Serve in cups; garnish with sour cream sprinkled with celery seeds.

BISQUES AND CREAM SOUPS

Chilled Springtime Soup
So easy and so refreshing! Made in a blender, it's creamy-smooth; in a mixer, tiny bits of the vegetables remain.
Makes 8 servings

Summer lifesavers guaranteed to cool down the hottest day in record time, this collection of ice-cold soups. Some are jellied, some creamed, some vegetable, some fish, some cheese, some simply seasoned meat broths.

1 can (10½ ounces) condensed cream of asparagus soup
1 soup can of water
⅔ cup milk
¼ cup chopped pared cucumber
1 tablespoon finely chopped green onion
½ teaspoon Worcestershire sauce

1 Combine all ingredients in an electric blender
or mixer; beat until creamy-smooth; chill several
hours.
2 Serve in chilled cups; float thinly sliced cucumber rind on top.

Guacamole Cream
Makes 4 to 6 servings

1 large avocado, peeled and pitted
1 slice onion
1 cup cream for whipping
1 envelope instant chicken broth
½ teaspoon salt
3 drops liquid red pepper seasoning
2 cups milk

1 Slice avocado into an electric-blender container; add onion and ½ cup cream. Cover; beat
until smooth.
2 Beat in remaining ingredients. Chill.
3 Pour into chilled cups or mugs. Sprinkle with
paprika, if you wish.

Curried Celery Soup
Makes 4 servings

½ cup finely diced celery
2 tablespoons butter or margarine
2 tablespoons all-purpose flour
1 teaspoon curry powder
1 teaspoon salt
¼ teaspoon pepper
1 cup skim milk
3 cups water

1 Sauté celery in butter or margarine in medium-size saucepan; remove from heat; blend
in flour, curry powder, salt and pepper; gradually stir in milk and water.
2 Cook, stirring constantly, until mixture
thickens slightly and begins to boil. Cover; simmer 10 minutes to blend flavors.

1844

Cucumber Cream
Makes 8 servings

3 large cucumbers
3 tablespoons butter or margarine
1 can (about 14 ounces) chicken broth
1 can (10¼ ounces) frozen condensed cream
 of potato soup, thawed
½ teaspoon salt
1 cup light cream or table cream

1 Pare cucumbers; quarter lengthwise; scoop
out seeds. Dice cucumbers.
2 Sauté in butter or margarine until soft in a
large saucepan. Pour mixture into an electric-
blender container; add chicken broth; cover.
Beat until smooth; pour back into saucepan.
3 Stir in potato soup, salt and cream. Heat
slowly to boiling.
4 Ladle into soup cups or small bowls; float a
thin slice of cucumber on each, if you wish.

Frosty Cucumber Soup
To fix this cool and refreshing summer soup
in a hurry, twirl it in your blender.
Makes 6 servings

2 cans (10½ ounces each) condensed cream
 of celery soup
1 small cucumber, pared and chopped
2 sprigs watercress, chopped
1 tablespoon chopped green onion
2 cups milk
½ cup dairy sour cream

1 Combine soup, cucumber, watercress and
green onion in large bowl of electric mixer; beat
until mixture turns pale green. (Or if using an
electric blender, twirl 1 can of soup at a time
and just slice in vegetables. Blender will do the
chopping.) Stir in milk; chill until serving time.
2 Spoon into mugs or soup bowls; top each
with a spoonful of sour cream; serve with bread
sticks, if you like.

Cucumber Cup
Cream of celery and chicken soups blend invit-
ingly with bits of tangy cucumber.
Makes 6 servings

1 can (10½ ounces) condensed cream of
 chicken soup
1 can (10½ ounces) condensed cream of celery
 soup
2 cups milk
1 medium-size cucumber

1 Combine soups and milk in a medium-size saucepan. Heat, stirring several times, to boiling; pour into a bowl.
2 Pare cucumber; quarter lengthwise, then slice thin; stir into soup; cover. Chill several hours, or overnight, until frosty-cold.
3 Pour into chilled bowls or cups; float a thin slice of cucumber on each serving, if you wish. (If you prefer soup smooth, beat in an electric blender just before serving.)

CHICKEN-MINT MEDLEY—Prepare recipe above, omitting cucumber. Just before serving, stir in 2 tablespoons finely chopped mint.

Potato-Cucumber Soup

It's like vichyssoise, with tiny cubes of crisp cucumber floating in it.
Makes 4 servings

1 can (10¼ ounces) frozen condensed cream
  of potato soup
2 cups milk
1 small cucumber, pared and finely diced
  (about 1 cup)
½ teaspoon salt
⅛ teaspoon pepper
2 tablespoons chopped parsley

1 Combine soup and milk in saucepan; heat to boiling; stirring often.
2 Remove from heat; stir in cucumber, salt and pepper; pour into medium-size bowl; chill.
3 Serve in cups or small bowls with parsley sprinkled on top.

Potato-Crab Bisque
Makes 4 servings

1 can (10¼ ounces) frozen cream of potato
  soup
2 cans milk
1 teaspoon grated onion
⅛ teaspoon curry powder
1 can (about 3¼ ounces) crabmeat, drained,
  boned and flaked
1 teaspoon chopped chives

1 Combine soup, milk, grated onion and curry powder in medium-size saucepan; heat just to boiling over medium heat, stirring often; pour into serving bowl; chill.
2 Just before serving, stir in crabmeat; sprinkle with chopped chives.

Dilled Mushroom Cream

A dash of dill and a smidgen of onion do great things for mushroom soup.
Makes 6 servings

1 package (2 cans) dry cream of mushroom
  soup mix
  OR: 2 envelopes cream of mushroom soup
  mix
2 teaspoons grated onion
2 teaspoons chopped fresh dill
  OR: 1 teaspoon dillweed
  Water and milk
2 tablespoons dairy sour cream
  Oyster crackers

1 Empty soup mix into medium-size saucepan; stir in onion and dill. Prepare with water and milk, following label directions.
2 While soup cooks, spoon a dab of sour cream on each oyster cracker; sprinkle with more dill, if you wish.
3 Pour soup into heated serving bowls; float several cream-topped crackers on each.

Mushroom Soup Supreme

Paper-thin slices of fresh mushrooms in rich bouillon make this dinner starter.
Makes 6 servings

½ pound fresh mushrooms
2 tablespoons butter or margarine
2 teaspoons lemon juice
1 tablespoon all-purpose flour
½ teaspoon salt
4 cups water
2 chicken-bouillon cubes
2 egg yolks
1 teaspoon sherry

1 Wash mushrooms; trim ends of stems, then cut through caps and stems to make thin slices.
2 Sauté, stirring often, in butter or margarine in a medium-size saucepan 2 minutes. Sprinkle with lemon juice; toss lightly to mix.
3 Blend in flour and salt; stir in water and bouillon cubes. Heat, stirring constantly until cubes dissolve, then cook until mixture boils 1 minute.
4 Beat egg yolks well with sherry in a small bowl; blend in about a half cup of the hot mushroom mixture, then stir back into remaining mixture in saucepan. Heat, stirring constantly, 1 minute longer.
5 Ladle soup into heated cups or bowls. Serve plain or with crisp crackers.

SOUP KETTLE

Double Mushroom Cream
Makes 6 servings

1 envelope mushroom soup mix
   OR: 1 can (2 to a package) dry cream of mushroom soup mix
2 cups water
1 can (3 or 4 ounces) chopped mushrooms
1 cup milk

1 Prepare soup mix with water in saucepan, following label directions.
2 Combine soup and mushrooms and liquid in electric-blender container; cover; beat until smooth. (If you prefer soup with pieces of mushrooms, no need to blend.) Return to saucepan; stir in milk; heat slowly to boiling.
3 Ladle into heated cups or bowls; float a few puffs of crisp popped corn on each, if you wish.

Creamy Spinach Cooler
Makes 6 servings

1 package (10 ounces) frozen chopped spinach
2 tablespoons butter or margarine
3 tablespoons all-purpose flour
1 envelope instant chicken broth
   OR: 1 teaspoon granulated chicken bouillon
½ teaspoon salt
⅛ teaspoon pepper
2 cups milk
1 large can (14½ ounces) evaporated milk
1 small onion, chopped fine (¼ cup)
1 tablespoon lemon juice

1846

1 Unwrap spinach; let stand at room temperature while making sauce.
2 Melt butter or margarine in a medium-size saucepan; stir in flour, chicken broth, salt and pepper; cook, stirring constantly, until bubbly. Stir in milk and evaporated milk; continue cooking and stirring until sauce thickens and boils 1 minute. Remove from heat.
3 Cut partly thawed spinach into ½-inch pieces; stir into hot sauce until completely thawed. Stir in onion and lemon juice. (If you prefer a smoother mixture, pour soup into an electric-blender container; cover. Beat until smooth.) Pour soup into a large bowl; cover. Chill several hours, or overnight.
4 Ladle into cups or small bowls. Garnish each with a sprig of watercress.

Creamy Tomato-Clam Soup
Makes 4 servings

1 can (10¾ ounces) condensed tomato soup
1 cup buttermilk
1 teaspoon Worcestershire sauce
¼ teaspoon salt
1 can (about 8 ounces) minced clams

1 Beat tomato soup with buttermilk, Worcestershire sauce and salt until smooth in a large bowl. Stir in clams and liquid; cover. Chill several hours or overnight.
2 Ladle into cups or small bowls; garnish each serving with a sprig of parsley, if you wish.

Tomato Cream Frost
Makes 8 servings

2 cans (about 1 pound each) stewed tomatoes
1 envelope unflavored gelatin
1 tablespoon sugar
1 tablespoon Worcestershire sauce
1 tablespoon lemon juice
1 cup cream

1 Drain juice from tomatoes into a medium-size saucepan; sprinkle gelatin over top. Heat, stirring constantly, until gelatin dissolves; remove from heat.
2 Cut tomatoes into small pieces; stir into gelatin mixture with sugar, Worcestershire sauce and lemon juice; stir in cream. Pour into a pan, 9x9x2.
3 Freeze until firm about 2 inches from edges but still soft in middle; spoon into a large bowl. Beat vigorously until smooth; return to pan. Freeze several hours longer, or until firm.
4 When ready to serve, beat again; spoon into parfait or sherbet glasses. Garnish each with a few small romaine leaves, if you wish.

Cream of Watercress Soup
Makes 6 servings

1 bunch watercress
1 tablespoon all-purpose flour
3 cups milk
1 teaspoon instant minced onion
1 teaspoon salt

1 Wash and dry watercress; save 6 sprigs for

garnish. Chop remaining stems and leaves (you should have about 1¾ cups).

2 Smooth flour and 1 to 2 tablespoons milk to a paste in medium-size saucepan; slowly stir in remaining milk; add onion and salt. Cook, stirring constantly, until mixture thickens slightly and boils 1 minute.

3 Remove from heat; stir in watercress. Serve at once or keep hot over very low heat. Do not let it boil. (If you prefer the soup puréed, twirl it in an electric blender.) Ladle into heated cups; garnish each with a sprig of watercress.

Creamy Watercress and Leek Soup

This pungent green adds its own special tang to cream of leek soup—and your blender is your mixer.
Makes 6 servings

½ bunch watercress
1 envelope (2 to a package) cream of leek soup
1 cup water
2 cups light cream or table cream
½ cup milk

1 Wash and dry watercress; remove leaves. (There should be about 1 cup.)

2 Blend soup mix with water in a small saucepan; heat to boiling; simmer 5 minutes.

3 Combine with watercress, cream and milk in an electric-blender container; cover. Beat at high speed 1 minute, or until creamy-smooth. (Or chop leaves fine, then stir into remaining ingredients in a large bowl.) Cover; chill until serving time.

4 Pour into stemmed glasses or cups; garnish with watercress, if you wish.

Country Buttermilk Soup

This tart and refreshing soup will make fans of many who say they don't like buttermilk.
Makes 4 servings

2 cups buttermilk
2 cups mixed vegetable juice (from a 46-ounce can)
1 tablespoon sugar
½ teaspoon salt
½ teaspoon instant onion powder
Few sprigs of watercress

1 Combine all ingredients except watercress in medium-size bowl or pitcher; beat to mix well; chill. (If you have an electric blender, use it to make this soup even faster.)

2 Serve in glasses or cups (it's thin enough to drink); garnish with watercress.

Cream Consommé

A smidgen of curry powder adds a subtle—and delightful—flavor touch.
Makes 8 servings

2 small apples
1 medium-size onion, chopped (½ cup)
⅛ teaspoon curry powder
2 tablespoons butter or margarine
2 cans (10½ ounces each) condensed beef consommé
1 cup cream for whipping

1 Pare one of the apples; halve, core, and chop. Sauté with onion and curry powder in butter or margarine until onion is soft in a medium-size saucepan.

2 Spoon into an electric-blender container; add 1 can of the consommé; cover. Beat at high speed several minutes, or until smooth. Pour back into saucepan.

3 Stir in remaining can of consommé and cream. Heat slowly until hot.

4 Ladle into heated soup cups or bowls. Quarter remaining apple; core; slice thin. Float 1 or 2 slices in each cup.

Note: If you do not have a blender, mince the one apple and onion; sauté with curry powder in butter or margarine, then heat with both cans of consommé and cream.

Jiffy Cheese Soup

Just heat two cans of ready-to-go soups with cheese—and supper's on!
Makes 4 servings

1 can (10¾ ounces) condensed cream of vegetable soup
1 can (10½ ounces) condensed chicken noodle soup
1 soup can of water
1 soup can of milk
1 cup grated process American cheese
¼ teaspoon Worcestershire sauce

1 Combine all ingredients in a large heavy saucepan. Heat slowly, stirring often, until cheese melts and soup is creamy. (Do not let it boil.)

2 Ladle into soup bowls; sprinkle with chopped parsley, if you wish.

1847

Hot Weather Cheddar Soup
Makes 6 to 8 servings

2 cans (10½ ounces each) condensed cream
  of celery soup
1 cup water
1 cup milk
1 jar (8 ounces) process Cheddar cheese
  spread
1 cup light cream or table cream
¼ teaspoon pepper

1 Blend celery soup, water and milk in a medium-size saucepan. Heat slowly, stirring several times, to boiling; remove from heat.
2 Stir in cheese until blended, then cream and pepper. Pour into a medium-size bowl; cover. Chill several hours or overnight.
3 Ladle into cups or small bowls. Garnish each serving with a spoonful of unsweetened whipped cream, shredded Cheddar cheese and a dash of paprika, if you wish.

Classic Clam Bisque
Makes 6 servings

1 medium-size onion, chopped (½ cup)
3 tablespoons (¾ stick) butter or margarine
3 tablespoons all-purpose flour
2 cans (8 ounces each) minced clams
1 bottle (8 ounces) clam juice
1½ cups light cream or table cream
1 tablespoon tomato paste (from a 6-ounce
  can)
4 teaspoons lemon juice

1 Sauté onion until soft in butter or margarine in a large saucepan; stir in flour; cook, stirring constantly, just until bubbly.
2 Stir in clams and liquid and clam juice; continue cooking and stirring until mixture thickens and boils 1 minute; cover. Simmer 15 minutes to blend flavors.
3 Blend in cream, tomato paste and lemon juice. Heat slowly just until hot.
4 Ladle into soup cups.
Note: If you prefer bisque smooth, pour mixture from Step 2 into an electric-blender container; cover. Beat until creamy-smooth; return to saucepan and stir in remaining ingredients, following directions in Step 3. To avoid last-minute fussing, soup may be made ahead, chilled, and reheated slowly just before serving.

1848

Quick Clam Bisque
A quick-to-make chilled soup that's hearty yet refreshing. Try it hot in winter, too.
Makes 4 servings

1 can (8 ounces) minced clams, drained and
  rinsed*
2 tablespoons butter or margarine
1 can (10¾ ounces) condensed vegetable soup
1 cup light cream or table cream
2 tablespoons chopped parsley
  Dash of cayenne

1 Sauté clams lightly in butter or margarine in medium-size saucepan.
2 Remove from heat; blend in soup and cream until smooth; stir in parsley and cayenne; pour into serving bowl; chill.

* We suggest rinsing clams, as the juice may make the soup too salty.

Oyster Cream
This version of popular oyster stew really hits the spot on a sizzling day.
Makes 6 servings

1 can (10¼ ounces) condensed oyster stew
1 can (10½ ounces) condensed cream of
  mushroom soup
2 cups milk
2 tablespoons chopped parsley

1 Combine soups and milk in an electric-blender container; cover. Beat until smooth; pour into a medium-size saucepan.
2 Heat slowly, stirring several times, just to boiling; pour into a bowl. Stir in parsley; cover. Chill several hours, or overnight, until frosty-cold.
3 Pour into chilled bowls or cups; garnish each serving with a sprig of parsley, if you wish.
  SEAFOOD BISQUE—Thaw either 1 can (10 ounces) condensed frozen lobster langostino bisque or 1 can (10 ounces) condensed frozen cream of shrimp soup, following label directions. Combine with 1 can (10½ ounces) condensed cream of mushroom soup and 3 cups milk. Prepare, following directions above.

Curried Shrimp Bisque
For this refreshing appetizer, combine frozen soup, cream and seasoning—and let your blender do the rest.
Makes 6 servings

2 cans (10 ounces each) frozen condensed
  cream of shrimp soup, thawed
2 cups light cream or table cream
½ teaspoon curry powder

1 Combine all ingredients, half at a time, in an electric-blender container; cover; beat until smooth. Chill several hours, or until serving time.
2 Pour into dainty cups or goblets; sprinkle lightly with a few finely cut chives, if you wish.

Frosty Fish Bisque
Makes 8 servings

1 package (1 pound) frozen perch fillets
1 teaspoon seasoned salt
1 bay leaf
2 slices lemon
1 cup water
2 cans (10¼ ounces each) frozen condensed cream of potato soup, thawed slightly
2 cups milk
1 cup light cream or table cream

1 Combine frozen fish, seasoned salt, bay leaf, lemon slices and water in a medium-size frying pan. Heat to boiling; cover. Simmer 10 minutes, or until fish flakes easily; remove bay leaf and lemon slices.
2 Break fish into pieces; place fish and cooking liquid in an electric-blender container; cover. Beat until smooth; pour into a large bowl. (If you do not have a blender, flake fish very fine with a fork, then mix with cooking liquid. Soup won't be as smooth but will taste just as good.)
3 While fish cooks, combine potato soup with 1 cup of the milk in a medium-size saucepan; heat, stirring several times, just to boiling. Cool slightly; pour into an electric-blender container; cover. Beat until smooth. Stir into fish mixture with remaining 1 cup milk and cream; cover. Chill several hours or overnight.
4 Ladle into cups or small bowls; float a thin green-pepper ring and several fish-shape crackers on each serving.

VEGETABLE SOUPS

Black Bean Soup
This soup is a take-off on the exotic Brazilian *Feijoada*. Tangy pieces of orange complement bits of hot pepperoni in a deep dark bean stock.
Makes 12 servings

4 cups dried black turtle beans (from two 1-pound bags)
3½ quarts water
½ pound pepperoni, cut into ½-inch pieces
3 large onions, sliced (3 cups)
1 boneless smoked pork butt (about 2 pounds)
2 cups dry red wine
3 oranges, peeled and sectioned
2 teaspoons salt
¼ cup chopped parsley

1 Combine beans with water in a large kettle; heat to boiling and boil 2 minutes; cover. Remove from heat; let stand 1 hour.
2 Heat beans to boiling again; add pepperoni and onions; reduce heat; cover. Simmer 2 hours, stirring occasionally, or until beans are tender. Add pork and wine. Simmer 1¼ hours longer, or until meat is cooked through.
3 Remove meat and keep warm. With a slotted spoon, remove pieces of sausage and about 3 cups of whole beans. Purée remaining beans in soup in a blender or press through a sieve. Return to kettle along with sausage and the whole beans.
4 Add sections from 2 of the oranges and salt. Taste; add additional salt, if you wish. Bring to boiling; ladle into soup bowls. Garnish each serving with a section of reserved orange; sprinkle with parsley.
5 Slice pork butt thin and pass it around to eat, on a separate plate, with mustard and whole-wheat bread.
Note: This freezes well. (Freeze soup and meats separately.)

Curried Black Bean Soup
Makes 4 to 6 servings

1 can (10½ ounces) condensed black-bean soup
1⅓ cups cold water
¼ teaspoon curry powder
¼ teaspoon grated lemon peel

1 Combine all ingredients in an electric-blender container or in a bowl; beat until smooth. Chill.
2 Pour into chilled glasses or cups. Garnish with lemon slices and sieved hard-cooked egg, if you wish.

Supper Bean Soup
Simmer a meaty ham bone with a pound of limas for a great whole-meal soup.
Makes 6 generous servings

SOUP KETTLE

1 pound dried large lima beans
7 cups water
1 meaty bone from baked ham
1 medium-size onion, diced (½ cup)
1 teaspoon salt
¼ teaspoon pepper
1 to 2 cups milk

1 Wash beans and pick over; combine with water in a kettle. Heat to boiling; cook 2 minutes; cover. Remove from heat; let stand 1 hour.
2 Add ham bone, onion, salt and pepper; heat to boiling again; cover tightly. Simmer 1½ hours, or until beans are tender.
3 Remove ham bone and cool until easy to handle. Strip off meat, removing any fat; dice meat; return to kettle.
4 Stir in 1 to 2 cups milk, depending on how thick you like soup; heat slowly to boiling.
5 Ladle into soup bowls; sprinkle with chopped parsley and serve with French bread, if you wish.

Old-Fashioned Lentil Soup
Ham bone plus the last meaty pickings from it go into this thick hearty soup.
Makes 6 servings

1 ham bone (from baked ham)
6 cups water
1¼ cups dried lentils (from a 1-pound package)
4 medium-size carrots, pared and sliced
1 large onion, chopped (1 cup)
2 teaspoons salt
1 teaspoon sugar
¼ teaspoon pepper
1 bay leaf

1 Combine all ingredients in a kettle; cover. Heat to boiling, then simmer 1 hour, or until lentils are tender.
2 Take out ham bone; strip off bits of meat and add to soup. Remove bay leaf.
3 Ladle soup into heated serving bowls.

1850

Smoky Pea Potage
Handy canned soup is the starter to combine with smoky wieners and carrots.
Makes 6 servings

½ pound (about 4) frankfurters, sliced ½ inch thick
1 cup diced, pared carrots
1 teaspoon salt
1 teaspoon leaf marjoram, crumbled
3 cups water
2 cans (11¼ ounces each) condensed green-pea soup

1 Sauté frankfurters lightly in a kettle; stir in carrots, salt, marjoram and water; cover. Simmer 15 minutes, or until carrots are tender.
2 Stir in green-pea soup; simmer, stirring several times, 15 minutes longer to blend flavors.
3 Ladle into soup bowls; garnish with paper-thin slices of raw carrot, if you wish.

Mushroom Soup, Country Style
Makes 4 servings

2½ cups milk
1 medium-size onion, finely chopped (½ cup)
1 cup chopped fresh mushrooms
¼ teaspoon salt
¼ teaspoon celery salt
¼ teaspoon paprika

1 Scald milk and onion in top of 1½-quart double boiler.
2 Add mushrooms and seasonings; place over boiling water; cook about 20 minutes, or until mushrooms are tender.
3 Serve piping hot, with chopped parsley and mushroom slices, if desired.

Onion Soup
This soup can be made ahead of time; reheat and add bread and cheese just before serving.
Makes 6 servings

4 large onions, sliced (1½ pounds)
4 tablespoons (½ stick) butter or margarine
6 cups BASIC BEEF STOCK (see index for recipe page number)
2 teaspoons salt
¼ teaspoon pepper
6 to 8 slices French bread, toasted
½ cup grated Parmesan cheese
¼ cup Gruyère or Swiss cheese

1 Sauté onion in butter or margarine in Dutch oven 15 minutes, or until lightly browned. Stir in BEEF STOCK, salt and pepper. Bring to boiling; reduce heat; cover; simmer 30 minutes.
2 Ladle soup into 6 ovenproof soup bowls or 12-ounce custard cups, or an 8-cup casserole. Lay bread slices on top, sprinkle with cheeses.
3 Heat in very hot oven (425°) 10 minutes, then place under preheated broiler and broil until top is bubbly and lightly browned.

Spinach Chowder
Makes 6 servings

1 package (10 ounces) frozen chopped spinach
2 cans (13 ounces each) vichyssoise
1 cup mhlk
2 envelopes instant chicken broth
  OR: 2 teaspoons granulated chicken bouillon
1 tablespoon instant minced onion
4 hard-cooked eggs, shelled and sliced

1 Combine frozen spinach, vichyssoise, milk, chicken broth and onion in large heavy saucepan or Dutch oven.
2 Heat *slowly,* stirring occasionally, about 20 minutes, or until spinach is thawed; cover. Simmer 5 minutes.
3 Ladle into soup bowls; garnish each with egg slices. Serve with cheese crackers, if you wish.

Potato Tureen Treat
Canned potato soup and cream-style corn blend in this so-good chowder.
Makes 4 servings

1 can (10½ ounces) condensed cream of potato soup
1 can (8 ounces) cream-style corn
1 cup evaporated milk (from a tall can)
1 cup milk
1 tablespoon grated onion
1 teaspoon Worcestershire sauce
¼ teaspoon pepper
1 tablespoon chopped parsley

Combine all ingredients except parsley; heat until bubbly hot. Pour into a tureen; sprinkle with parsley.

Tomato Frappé
Makes 6 servings

6 large ripe tomatoes, chopped
1½ teaspoons salt
⅛ teaspoon pepper
⅛ teaspoon ground thyme
3 whole cloves
1 large bay leaf
½ teaspoon onion juice
1 tablespoon lemon juice
  Cucumber slices

1 Combine tomatoes, salt, pepper, thyme, cloves, bay leaf and onion juice in a medium-size saucepan. Heat to boiling; cover. Cook 20 minutes.
2 Press mixture through a fine sieve into a medium-size bowl; stir in lemon juice. Pour into a shallow pan, 9x9x2; freeze several hours, or until firm.
3 Just before serving, break up frozen soup; crush fine in an ice crusher or an electric blender. (Or place pieces in a double-thick transparent bag; crush with a mallet.)
4 Spoon into cups or small bowls; garnish each serving with several cucumber slices.

Easy Gazpacho
Here's a speedy version of popular Spanish gazpacho, with its variety of toppings.
Makes 6 servings

1 can (10¾ ounces) condensed tomato soup
1 soup can of water
3½ cups mixed vegetable juice (from a 46-ounce can)
1 tablespoon lemon juice
1 teaspoon seasoned salt
¼ cup sliced pitted ripe olives
1 cup croutons
1 cup grated raw carrots
1 cup diced avocado
1 cup sliced green onions

1 Blend tomato soup, water, vegetable juice, lemon juice and seasoned salt in large bowl; chill several hours, as the soup tastes best when served frosty-cold.
2 To serve, pour soup into a big glass or pottery bowl; stir in ripe-olive slices. (If you have a second larger bowl, partly fill with crushed ice and set soup bowl in it to keep chilly-cold. Surround with smaller bowls of croutons, carrots, avocado and green onions. Spoon soup into serving cups; let each person add the topping he likes best.

Alpine Tomato Appetizer
Your helpers for this nippy starter: Dip mix and canned colorful mixed vegetables.
Makes 6 servings

1 envelope unflavored gelatin
3 cups tomato juice (from a 46-ounce can)
1 envelope (about 1 tablespoon) onion-dip mix
1 can (1 pound) mixed vegetables, drained

1851

½ cup chopped green pepper
6 tablespoons dairy sour cream

1 Combine gelatin and 1 cup tomato juice in small saucepan; heat slowly, stirring constantly, just until gelatin dissolves. Pour into medium-size bowl.
2 Stir in remaining tomato juice, dip mix, vegetables and green pepper. Chill about 2 hours, or until set. (Mixture will be soft.)
3 Spoon into individual serving dishes; top each with 1 tablespoon sour cream and a green-pepper twist, if you wish. (To make: Shave paper-thin strips from cut edge of a green pepper with a vegetable parer; tie each into a loose knot.)

Double Tomato Soup
Makes 4 servings

1 medium-size onion, chopped (½ cup)
2 tablespoons butter or margarine
3 medium-size tomatoes, diced (about 2 cups)
½ cup diced celery
1 can (10¾ ounces) condensed tomato soup
1 soup can water
1 teaspoon sugar
½ teaspoon salt
½ teaspoon leaf basil, crumbled
⅛ teaspoon pepper

1 Sauté onion in butter or margarine until soft in medium-size saucepan.
2 Stir in remaining ingredients; heat to boiling. Simmer, uncovered, stirring once or twice, 10 minutes, to blend flavors.
3 Spoon into heated soup bowls; float a few croutons on top of each, if you wish.

Cheese and Vegetable Chowder
Makes 6 servings

4 medium-size potatoes, pared and diced (3 cups)
1 medium-size onion, chopped (½ cup)
3 large stalks celery, trimmed and sliced thin
2 large carrots, pared and sliced thin
¼ green pepper, seeded and chopped
2½ cups water
2 teaspoons salt
Dash of pepper
2 cups milk
1 package (8 ounces) process American cheese, shredded (2 cups)
3 frankfurters, sliced thin
Paprika

1 Combine potatoes, onion, celery, carrots,

green pepper, water, salt and pepper in a kettle; heat to boiling; cover. Simmer 20 minutes, or until vegetables are tender.
2 Stir in milk, cheese and frankfurters. Heat slowly, stirring constantly, until cheese melts.
3 Ladle into heated soup bowls or plates; sprinkle each with paprika.

Creamy Corn Chowder
Makes 2 quarts

¼ pound lean salt pork
1 large onion, chopped (1 cup)
1 cup diced celery
2 tablespoons butter or margarine
1 cup water
2 cans (about 1 pound each) cream-style corn
2 cups fresh milk
1 large can (14½ ounces) evaporated milk
¼ teaspoon salt
Dash of pepper

1 Dice salt pork finely; sauté slowly in kettle 15 minutes, or until crisp and golden; spoon from kettle with slotted spoon; drain on paper towels; save for Step 3. Pour all fat from kettle, but do not wash kettle.
2 Sauté onion and celery in butter or margarine in same kettle for 5 minutes; add water; cover; simmer 5 minutes.
3 Stir in corn, fresh and evaporated milk, cooked salt pork, salt and pepper. (Salt pork varies in saltiness, so season lightly until you have tasted chowder.)
4 Heat chowder just to boiling; serve with buttered toasted pilot or unsalted plain crackers.

Spoon-Up Fresh Vegetable Soup
Makes about 12 cups

1 pound lean shin or chuck beef, cut in 1-inch cubes
1 beef knucklebone, cracked
6 cups water
2 cans (about 1 pound each) tomatoes
3 carrots, sliced
1 leek or onion, sliced
1 clove of garlic, minced
2 bay leaves
1 tablespoon sugar
2 teaspoons salt
2 cups chopped cabbage
1 cup sliced zucchini
1 cup cut-up green beans

1 cup broken macaroni
¼ cup chopped parsley
Grated Parmesan cheese

1 Simmer beef and bone with water, tomatoes, carrots, leek or onion, garlic, bay leaves, sugar and salt in kettle about 3 hours; remove bone; cool slightly; skim off fat.
2 Add cabbage, zucchini, green beans and macaroni; cook 45 minutes longer, or until beans are tender; sprinkle with parsley; serve with grated cheese.

Duchess Vegetable Soup
Garden-fresh sweet peas add color and crunch to creamy-rich cheese soup from a can.
Makes 6 servings

1 medium-size onion, chopped (½ cup)
1 cup diced celery
2 tablespoons butter or margarine
2½ cups water
2 tablespoons instant mashed potato (from a package)
1 pound fresh peas, shelled (1 cup)
1 can (10¾ ounces) condensed cheese soup
⅛ teaspoon pepper
1 teaspoon Worcestershire sauce

1 Sauté onion and celery in butter or margarine until softened in medium-size saucepan; stir in water; heat to boiling.
2 Stir in instant mashed potato until blended, then add peas. Cover; cook 5 minutes. Stir in remaining ingredients until well blended; heat just to boiling.
3 Pour into mugs or soup bowls; float a few fluffs of popped corn on each serving for a snowy garnish, if you wish.

Garden Salad-Soup
Drink your salad as a cold summer soup. Also good hot on a rainy day.
Makes 6 servings

1 small onion, chopped (¼ cup)
½ teaspoon leaf basil, crumbled
2 tablespoons butter or margarine
1 cup water
2 teaspoons instant chicken bouillon
  OR: 2 chicken-bouillon cubes
1 teaspoon sugar
1 teaspoon Worcestershire sauce
2 cups finely chopped romaine or iceberg lettuce

1 cup finely chopped cabbage
1 cup finely chopped spinach
3 cups tomato juice (from a 46-ounce can)

1 Sauté onion with basil in butter or margarine until soft in medium-size saucepan; stir in water, instant chicken bouillon or cubes, sugar and Worcestershire sauce; heat, stirring until bouillon is dissolved; remove from heat.
2 Combine remaining ingredients in large bowl; stir in bouillon mixture; chill.

El Rancho Soup
Makes 4 servings

1 tablespoon butter or margarine
1 small onion, chopped
1 cup Frenched green beans, cut in 1-inch pieces
¼ teaspoon sugar
1 can (10½ ounces) chicken noodle soup
1 can (10½ ounces) condensed beef bouillon
2 soup cans of water
2 tablespoons chopped parsley
1 pimiento, diced
1 ear of corn, cut in 1-inch-thick slices

1 Melt butter or margarine in large saucepan; add onion, beans and sugar; sauté over low heat 2 to 3 minutes, stirring often.
2 Stir in soups, water, parsley, pimiento and corn; heat to boiling; simmer 5 minutes, or until beans are cooked tender-crisp.

Vegetable Minestrone
Makes 4 to 6 servings

1 envelope (2½ ounces) tomato-vegetable soup mix
3 cups boiling water
1 medium-size onion, chopped
1 can (about 1 pound) red kidney beans
1 can (12 to 16 ounces) whole-kernel corn
1 can (8 ounces) tomato sauce
1 teaspoon salt
⅛ teaspoon pepper
½ cup chopped parsley
  Grated Parmesan cheese

1853

1 Stir soup mix into boiling water in large saucepan; add onion, kidney beans, corn, tomato sauce, salt and pepper; cover.
2 Heat to boiling; cook 10 minutes, or until onion is tender; stir in parsley; serve in mugs or bowls with a generous sprinkling of Parmesan cheese.

HEARTY MAIN-DISH SOUPS AND CHOWDERS

Boothbay Chowder
Makes 6 to 8 servings

3 slices bacon, chopped
1 large onion, chopped (1 cup)
4 medium-size potatoes, pared and diced (3 cups)
2 cups water
1 teaspoon salt
¼ teaspoon pepper
2 cans (10½ ounces each) minced clams
1 bottle (8 ounces) clam juice
1 cup light cream or table cream
3 tablespoons all-purpose flour
2 tablespoons minced parsley

1 Cook bacon until crisp in a large heavy saucepan or Dutch oven. Remove bacon with slotted spoon; drain on paper toweling; reserve. Add onion to bacon drippings in saucepan; sauté until soft.
2 Add potatoes, water, salt and pepper; cover. Simmer, 15 minutes, or until potatoes are tender. Remove from heat.
3 Drain liquid from clams into a 4-cup measure; reserve clams. Add bottled clam juice and cream.
4 Briskly stir flour into clam liquid in cup. Add to potato mixture in saucepan. Cook, stirring constantly, over medium heat, until chowder thickens and bubbles 1 minute.
5 Add clams; heat just until piping-hot. Ladle into soup bowls. Sprinkle with parsley and reserved bacon. Serve with pilot crackers, if you wish.

1854

Tureen Shrimps
Frozen potato soup, shrimps and cheese go into this companylike surprise.
Makes 6 servings

1 large onion, chopped (1 cup)
2 tablespoons butter or margarine
2 cans (10¼ ounces each) frozen potato soup, thawed
3½ cups milk
1 package (1 pound) frozen deveined shelled raw shrimps
½ cup grated American cheese
2 tablespoons chopped parsley

1 Sauté onion in butter or margarine until soft in a kettle; stir in potato soup and milk.
2 Heat to boiling; stir in frozen shrimps; heat to boiling again, then simmer, stirring several times, 25 minutes, or just until shrimps are tender. Remove from heat.
3 Just before serving, stir in grated cheese until melted. Ladle into soup bowls; sprinkle with parsley.

Crab-Cheese Chowder
Makes 4 to 6 servings

1½ tablespoons butter or margarine
1 onion, thinly sliced
2 stalks of celery, thinly sliced
3 cups diced raw potatoes
½ cup water
1 teaspoon salt
¼ teaspoon pepper
¼ pound process cheese
1 can (about 6 ounces) crabmeat, boned and flaked
3 cups milk, scalded
1 tablespoon chopped parsley

1 Melt butter or margarine in large saucepan; add onion and celery; cook slowly until golden; add potatoes, water, salt and pepper; simmer 15 to 20 minutes, or until potatoes are tender.
2 Slice in cheese; add crabmeat, milk and parsley; heat slowly until cheese melts. For a party touch, sprinkle more chopped parsley in wreath on top.

Oyster Chowder
Makes 6 generous servings

1 can (1 pound) small white potatoes, drained and diced
4 tablespoons (½ stick) butter or margarine
2 cans (10¼ ounces each) condensed oyster stew
1 can (1 pound) green peas
1 can (12 or 16 ounces) whole-kernel corn
1 can (5 ounces) lobster meat, drained and diced
2 cups milk
2 tablespoons instant minced onion
1 teaspoon salt
1 teaspoon Worcestershire sauce
Few drops liquid red pepper seasoning
Chopped parsley

1 Sauté potatoes lightly in butter or margarine in a kettle.
2 Stir in oyster stew, peas and corn and liquids, lobster, milk, onion, salt, Worcestershire sauce

Boothbay Chowder is a New-England-style clam chowder made with potatoes, onions, bacon, parsley and cream.

Summer Fish Chowder is chock full of cod and lobster, clams, cream-style corn, frozen green peas and milk.

1856

and red pepper seasoning; heat very slowly just to boiling. (Do not let chowder boil.)
3 Ladle into a tureen or heated soup bowls: sprinkle with chopped parsley. Serve with thin bread sticks, slices of crusty bread or your favorite crackers, if you wish.

●

Classic Oyster Stew
The Yankee way with stew—and so easy to make!
Makes 4 servings

    2 cups milk
    2 cups light cream or table cream
    ½ teaspoon salt
    ¼ teaspoon paprika
    1 pint (about 24) oysters
      OR: 2 cans (7 ounces each) frozen oysters, thawed
    4 tablespoons (½ stick) butter or margarine

1 Scald milk with cream in medium-size saucepan over low heat (do not boil); stir in salt and paprika.
2 Heat oysters and juice in butter or margarine until edges of oysters begin to curl in medium-size saucepan; stir in scalded-milk mixture.
3 Ladle into heated soup bowls or mugs. Serve with oyster crackers, if you wish.

MAIN DISH SOUPS AND CHOWDERS

Creole Fish Soup
Makes 5 cups

1 small onion, sliced
½ cup sliced celery
1 teaspoon chili powder
1 tablespoon olive oil
2 cans (8 ounces each) tomato sauce
1 cup water
1 teaspoon salt
1 teaspoon sugar
¼ teaspoon Worcestershire sauce
1 package (12 ounces) frozen fish fillets (cod, sole, haddock, perch, whiting)
2 cups hot cooked rice
2 tablespoons chopped parsley

1 Sauté onion, celery and chili powder lightly in oil in large saucepan 10 minutes; stir in tomato sauce, water, salt, sugar and Worcestershire sauce; heat to boiling.
2 Add frozen fish in one piece; simmer, separating it with a fork as it thaws, 15 minutes, or until it flakes easily.
3 Spoon into chowder bowls; top each with a mound of rice mixed with parsley.

Summer Fish Chowder
It's a seafood fan's dream with cod, whole clams and lobster, plus two vegetables.
Makes 6 servings

1 large onion, chopped (1 cup)
3 tablespoons butter or margarine
1 package (1 pound) frozen cod fillets
1 package (10 ounces) frozen peas
2 cups water
2 teaspoons salt
¼ teaspoon pepper
¼ teaspoon leaf thyme, crumbled
1 can (about 5 ounces) lobster meat
2 cans (about 10 ounces each) whole clams
1 can (1 pound) cream-style corn
1 tall can (14½ ounces) evaporated milk
Chopped parsley

1 Sauté onion in butter or margarine until soft in a kettle; add frozen cod, peas, water, salt, pepper and thyme; cover. Heat to boiling, then simmer, breaking cod into large flakes as it thaws, 15 minutes.
2 While fish simmers, drain lobster; remove bony tissue, if any, then cut meat into large pieces.
3 Stir into fish mixture in kettle with clams and broth, corn and evaporated milk; cover. Heat slowly just to boiling.
4 Ladle into heated soup bowls and sprinkle with chopped parsley.

Tureen Salmon
Makes 8 generous servings

3 medium-size potatoes, pared and diced (1½ cups)
1 large onion, chopped (1 cup)
1 cup thinly sliced celery
4 tablespoons (½ stick) butter or margarine
⅓ cup sifted all-purpose flour
6 cups milk
1 bag (2 pounds) frozen peas and carrots
2 cans (1 pound each) salmon
1 teaspoon dillweed
1½ teaspoons salt
¼ teaspoon seasoned pepper
Chowder crackers

1 Cook potatoes, covered, in boiling water to cover in a medium-size saucepan 15 minutes, or just until tender; set aside.
2 Sauté onion and celery in butter or margarine until soft in a kettle. Blend in flour; cook, stirring constantly, until bubbly. Stir in milk; continue cooking and stirring until mixture thickens and boils 1 minute.
3 Stir in peas and carrots; heat slowly to boiling; cover. Simmer 12 minutes, or until vegetables are tender.
4 Drain salmon; remove skin and bones; break salmon into large chunks. Stir into vegetable mixture with potatoes and liquid, dillweed, salt and pepper. Heat slowly, stirring several times, just until hot.
5 Ladle into a tureen or heated soup bowls or plates; sprinkle with more dillweed, if you wish, and serve with chowder crackers.

Tomato-Tuna Treat
Makes 6 servings

1 large onion, chopped (1 cup)
1 cup chopped celery
3 tablespoons butter or margarine
2 cans (7 ounces each) tuna
1 package (10 ounces) frozen peas
2 cups tomato juice
1 cup water
1 teaspoon salt
1 teaspoon sugar
1 teaspoon leaf basil, crumbled

1 Sauté onion and celery in butter or margarine until soft in a kettle.

1857

2 Drain tuna and break into chunks; stir into onion mixture with frozen peas, tomato juice, water, salt, sugar and basil; cover. Simmer 30 minutes to blend flavors.
3 Ladle into soup bowls; garnish with chopped parsley, if you wish.

Chowder Diamond Head
Makes 6 servings

      1 cup sliced celery
      1 small onion, chopped (¼ cup)
      2 tablespoons butter or margarine
      ½ teaspoon ground ginger
      2 cans (10½ ounces each) condensed cream
         of chicken soup
   1⅓ cups water
   1⅓ cups milk
      1 can (5 ounces) boned chicken, diced
      1 can (about 9 ounces) pineapple tidbits,
         drained
         Shredded coconut

1 Sauté celery and onion in butter or margarine until soft in a large heavy saucepan or Dutch oven; add ginger, blending thoroughly.
2 Stir in soup, water and milk. Add chicken and pineapple. Heat, stirring frequently, until bubbly-hot.
3 Ladle into soup bowls. Sprinkle with coconut. Serve with hot buttered rolls, if you wish.

Sunday Supper Chowder
Makes 6 servings

      1 medium-size onion, chopped (½ cup)
      2 stalks celery, sliced
      3 tablespoons butter or margarine
      2 tablespoons all-purpose flour
      ½ teaspoon salt
      ⅛ teaspoon pepper
      2 cups turkey broth*
      2 large carrots, pared and cut into thin rings
      1 package (10 ounces) frozen mixed vegeta-
         bles
      3 cups milk
      1 package (8 ounces) process American
         cheese, diced
      1 cup diced cooked turkey
      1 tablespoon chopped parsley

1 Sauté onion and celery slowly in butter or margarine in large kettle 5 minutes; remove from heat.

1858

2 Blend in flour, salt and pepper; gradually add turkey broth; heat, stirring constantly, until mixture comes to boiling.
3 Add carrots and frozen mixed vegetabless; cover; simmer 30 minutes, or until vegetables are tender; stir in milk, cheese, turkey and parsley.
4 Heat slowly, stirring often, until cheese melts and soup is piping-hot. (Do not let soup boil, as it may curdle.)

* To make turkey broth: Break up turkey carcass to fit into large saucepan; add 2 cups cold water, 1 sliced onion and a handful of celery tops; cover; simmer 1 hour. Strain broth; if needed, add enough water to make 2 cups.

Brunswick Stew
Chicken, canned soup and vegetables add up to this satisfying meal-in-a-bowl.
Makes 8 servings

      1 broiler-fryer, weighing about 2½ pounds,
         quartered
      5 teaspoons seasoned salt
         Water
      1 large onion, chopped (1 cup)
      2 tablespoons butter or margarine
      2 packages (10 ounces each) frozen Fordhook
         lima beans
      2 cans (10¾ ounces each) condensed tomato-
         rice soup
      2 cups thinly sliced celery
      2 cans (1 pound each) cream-style corn

1 Combine chicken, 3 teaspoons of the salt and 4 cups water in a kettle; cover. Simmer 45 minutes, or until chicken is tender. Take meat from bones; dice. Strain broth into a 4-cup measure; add water, if needed, to make 4 cups.
2 Sauté onion in butter or margarine until soft in same kettle; add lima beans, soup, two soup cans of water and celery; cover. Simmer 15 minutes, or until beans are tender. Stir in chicken, broth, corn and remaining 2 teaspoons seasoned salt.
3 Heat slowly just to boiling. Ladle into heated soup bowls.

Country Chicken Soup
Fast-cook broiler-fryer and cubes of beef go into this made-from-scratch hearty.
Makes 8 servings

   1½ pounds chuck beefsteak, cut into ½ inch
         cubes
      1 large onion, chopped (1 cup)

1 broiler-fryer, weighing 2½ to 3 pounds, quartered
1 cup chopped celery
2 teaspoons salt
1 teaspoon seasoned salt
½ teaspoon pepper
½ teaspoon leaf rosemary, crumbled
½ teaspoon leaf thyme, crumbled
1 bay leaf
10 cups water
2 cups uncooked medium noodles

1 Brown beef in its own fat in a kettle or Dutch oven; stir in onion and sauté lightly.
2 Add chicken, celery, salt, seasoned salt, pepper, rosemary, thyme, bay leaf and water to kettle; heat to boiling; cover. Simmer 1 hour, or until chicken is tender; remove from kettle. Continue cooking beef 20 minutes, or until tender; remove bay leaf.
3 While beef finishes cooking, pull skin from chicken and take meat from bones; cut meat in cubes. Return to kettle; heat to boiling.
4 Stir in noodles. Cook 10 minutes, or until noodles are tender.
5 Ladle into soup plates. Sprinkle with chopped parsley and serve with your favorite crisp crackers, if you wish.

Chicken Soup with Dumplings
A creamy-thick soup with tender little chicken balls and vegetables to munch.
Makes 6 servings

Chicken Dumplings
1 cup diced cooked chicken
1 cooked chicken liver
1 egg
⅓ cup sifted all-purpose flour
¼ cup milk
1 teaspoon salt
Dash of pepper
Dash of nutmeg
1 tablespoon chopped parsley
1 cup water
6 cups BASIC CHICKEN STOCK (see index for recipe page number)

Soup
¼ cup chopped green onion
¼ cup chicken fat, butter or margarine
¼ sifted all-purpose flour
1 package (10 ounces) frozen mixed vegetables
½ teaspoon salt
1½ cups diced cooked chicken

1 Combine chicken, liver, egg, flour, milk, salt,

pepper and nutmeg in blender; blend at high speed until smooth. Turn into small bowl, stir in parsley; cover.
2 Bring water and 1 cup of the CHICKEN STOCK to boiling in a large saucepan. Shape chicken mixture, one-half at a time, into ¾-inch balls with a teaspoon. Drop one by one into boiling stock. Simmer gently, uncovered, 8 to 10 minutes; remove with a slotted spoon; keep warm. Repeat with second half.
3 Sauté onion in chicken fat, or butter or margarine in kettle or Dutch oven, until soft but not brown, 3 to 4 minutes; stir in flour; gradually add remaining chicken stock, stirring constantly; bring to boiling; add vegetables and salt; cover. Cook 10 minutes, or until vegetables are tender.
4 Add chicken dumplings, cooking stock and chicken; heat 5 minutes. Ladle into soup bowls; serve with crusty bread.

Mulligatawny Soup
A classic soup, with origins in India, is richly flavored with exotic curry.
Makes 6 servings

3 medium carrots, pared and sliced
2 stalks of celery, sliced
6 cups BASIC CHICKEN STOCK (see index for recipe page number)
3 cups cooked diced chicken
1 large onion, chopped (1 cup)
4 tablespoons (½ stick) butter or margarine
1 apple, pared, quartered, cored and chopped
5 teaspoons curry powder
1 teaspoon salt
¼ cup sifted all-purpose flour
1 tablespoon lemon juice
2 cups hot cooked rice
¼ cup chopped parsley
6 lemon slices (optional)

1 Cook carrots and celery in 1 cup stock in a medium-size saucepan 20 minutes, or until tender. Add chicken; heat just until hot; cover; keep warm.
2 Sauté onion until soft in butter or margarine in Dutch oven; stir in apple, curry powder and salt; sauté 5 minutes longer, or until apple is soft; add flour. Gradually stir in remaining chicken stock; heat to boiling, stirring constantly; reduce heat; cover; simmer 15 minutes.
3 Add vegetables and chicken with the stock they were cooked in; bring just to boiling. Stir in lemon juice.
4 Ladle into soup plates or bowls; pass hot cooked rice and chopped parsley and lemon slices, if you wish, for each to add his own garnish. Good with crusty French bread.

1859

Golden Turkey Chowder
Makes 4 servings

2 cans (10½ ounces each) condensed golden mushroom soup
2 soup cans of milk
1 can (about 1 pound) cream-style corn
1 cup thinly sliced celery
1 tablespoon instant minced onion
⅛ teaspoon pepper
2 cans (5 ounces each) boned turkey, diced

1 Combine soup, milk, corn, celery, onion and pepper in a large saucepan. Heat slowly, stirring several times, to boiling, then simmer 3 minutes to blend flavors.
2 Stir in turkey. Ladle into a tureen or soup plates. Garnish with parsley and serve with bread sticks, if you wish.

Jambalaya Chowder
Makes 8 servings

1 medium-size onion, chopped (½ cup)
1 small green pepper, halved, seeded and diced
1 clove of garlic, crushed
2 tablespoons butter or margarine
2 cans (10½ ounces each) condensed chicken and rice soup
2⅔ cups water
2 large tomatoes, peeled and diced
1 small bay leaf
½ teaspoon chili powder
⅛ teaspoon ground thyme
1 package (about 8 ounces) frozen shelled deveined shrimps
1 can (5 ounces) cooked chicken, diced
1 package (6 ounces) cooked ham, cubed

1 Sauté onion, green pepper and garlic in butter or margarine until soft in a large heavy saucepan or Dutch oven. Stir in soup, water, tomatoes, bay leaf, chili powder and thyme. (For easy peeling, place tomatoes in boiling water for 30 seconds.) Cover; simmer 10 minutes. Remove bay leaf.
2 Stir in shrimps, chicken and ham; cover. Simmer 10 minutes longer, or until shrimps are tender. Ladle into soup bowls. Serve with buttered hot biscuits, if you wish.

Golden Turkey Chowder is a canned-food quickie made in less than five minutes. All you have to do is open five cans (two of golden mushroom soup, one of corn, two of turkey), slice a cup of celery, heat and stir.

Penn-Dutch Rivel Chowder
Makes 8 servings

4 medium-size potatoes, pared and sliced (3 cups)
1 large onion, sliced (1 cup)
3½ cups water
1¾ teaspoons salt
⅛ teaspoon pepper
1 egg
1 cup sifted all-purpose flour
1 can (about 4 ounces) deviled ham
1 quart milk

1 Combine potatoes, onions, water, 1¼ teaspoons of the salt and pepper in a large heavy saucepan or Dutch oven; cover. Simmer 15 minutes or until potatoes are tender; remove from heat.
2 To make rivels (tiny dumplings): Beat egg in medium-size bowl. Add remaining ½ teaspoon salt and flour; mix well to form a soft dough; reserve.
3 Stir ham and milk into potato mixture; beat just until bubbly; cover. Simmer 2 minutes.
4 Rub a small amount of dough between palms of hands over kettle of simmering chowder, allowing tiny pieces of dough to drop into soup, forming rivels. Simmer about 5 minutes, or until rivels are tender and soup is thickened.
5 Ladle into soup bowls. Serve with hot muffins, if you wish.

Winter's Best Soup
Makes 6 generous servings

3 three-inch beef marrow bones
1 beef knuckle bone, cracked
10 cups water
1 can (about 1 pound) tomatoes
3 medium-size carrots, pared and diced
2 small white turnips, pared and diced
1 medium-size onion, chopped
1 cup diced celery
6 whole cloves
1 bay leaf
⅛ teaspoon leaf thyme, crumbled
2 teaspoons salt
1 teaspoon sugar
¼ teaspoon pepper
1 cup dried lima beans
½ pound green beans, diced
1 cup shell macaroni
2 cups chopped raw spinach
MARROW BALLS (recipe follows)

1861

SOUP KETTLE

1 Remove marrow from marrow bones to make BALLS.

2 Combine bones and remaining ingredients, except lima and green beans, macaroni, spinach and MARROW BALLS, in large kettle.

3 Cover; simmer 1½ hours; add lima beans; cook 1 hour.

4 Remove bones, skim off fat; add green beans and macaroni; cover; cook 15 minutes; add spinach and MARROW BALLS; cover; cook 5 minutes.

Marrow Balls
Makes 24 marble-size balls

½ *cup mashed beef marrow (from beef marrow bones)*
1 *cup soft bread crumbs*
1 *egg, beaten*
1 *tablespoon minced parsley*
½ *teaspoon salt*
⅛ *teaspoon pepper*

Combine all ingredients in small bowl; form lightly into 24 balls.

Copenhagen Oxtail Soup
Savory oxtail soup takes on an elegant look, garnished with EGGS MIMOSA.
Bake at 450° for 45 minutes. Makes 6 servings

3 *pounds oxtails, cut up*
3 *teaspoons salt*
⅛ *teaspoon pepper*
1 *large onion, chopped (1 cup)*
2 *carrots, pared and sliced (1 cup)*
1 *parsnip, pared and sliced (¾ cup)*
1 *turnip, pared and sliced (1 cup)*
2 *tablespoons brandy*
6 *cups water*
½ *teaspoon leaf savory, crumbled*
1 *bay leaf*
  EGGS MIMOSA *(recipe follows)*
  Chopped parsley

1 Spread oxtails in a single layer in shallow roasting pan. Roast in very hot oven (450°) 45 minutes, or until nicely browned. Drain off fat, reserving 2 tablespoons.

2 Sauté onion, carrots, parsnip and turnip in reserved fat in kettle or Dutch oven, 10 minutes, or until soft. Add browned oxtails. Drizzle brandy over, ignite carefully with a lighted match. Add water to roasting pan in which oxtails were browned. Heat, stirring constantly, to dissolve browned bits; pour over oxtails and vegetables in Dutch oven; add savory and bay leaf. Bring to boiling; reduce heat; cover; simmer slowly 2 hours, or until meat separates easily from bones.

3 Ladle into soup bowls; place a half egg in each, sprinkle with parsley. Serve with crusty French bread.

EGGS MIMOSA—Cut 3 hard-cooked eggs in half lengthwise. Carefully remove yolks, keeping whites whole. Press yolks through a sieve, spoon back into whites.

Old-Fashioned Beef and Vegetable Soup
This hearty soup, chock-full of vegetables and meat, is a meal in itself.
Makes 8 servings

1½ *quarts BASIC BEEF STOCK (see index for recipe page number)*
2 *potatoes, peeled and diced (2 cups)*
2 *carrots, pared and sliced*
1 *cup sliced celery*
2 *small onions, peeled and quartered*
1 *can (1 pound) whole tomatoes*
2 *teaspoons salt*
⅛ *teaspoon pepper*
½ *head green cabbage, shredded (2 cups)*
1 *cup frozen corn (from a plastic bag)*
3 *cups diced cooked beef*
1 *tablespoon chopped parsley*

1 Heat BEEF STOCK to boiling in a large saucepan or kettle; add potatoes, carrots, celery, onions, tomatoes, salt and pepper; heat to boiling again; reduce heat; cover; simmer 20 minutes.

2 Stir in cabbage, corn and meat; simmer 10 minutes longer or just until all vegetables are crisply tender. Sprinkle with parsley.

3 Ladle into soup bowls. Serve with chunks of crusty bread.

Borsch
Adding grated fresh beets to soup just before serving gives a beautiful red color. May be served hot or chilled.
Makes 6 servings

2 *carrots, pared and sliced (1 cup)*
1½ *cups shredded raw beets*
1 *turnip, pared and diced (¾ cup)*
1 *medium-size onion, sliced*
1 *cup water*

2 tablespoons cider vinegar
2 teaspoons salt
1 teaspoon sugar
6 cups BASIC BEEF STOCK (see index for recipe page number)
2 cups diced cooked beef
½ small head of cabbage, shredded (3 cups)
Sour cream

1 In a kettle combine carrots, 1 cup beets, turnip, onion, water, vinegar, salt and sugar.
2 Bring to boiling; reduce heat, cover; simmer 20 minutes. Add BEEF STOCK, beef and cabbage. Simmer 10 to 15 minutes longer or until all vegetables are tender.
3 Stir in remaining ½ cup beets. Ladle into soup bowls. Serve with hearty chunks of homemade bread.

Meat Ball Chowder
Tiny balls of mint-seasoned beef and pork cook in a rich onion broth.
Makes 6 servings

¾ pound ground beef
¾ pound ground pork
1 egg
2 teaspoons dried mint leaves, crushed
1½ teaspoons salt
⅛ teaspoon pepper
4 cups water
1 can or 1 envelope onion soup mix
1 can (about 1 pound) stewed tomatoes
1 can (about 1 pound) red kidney beans
¼ cup chopped parsley

1 Mix ground beef and pork with egg, mint leaves, salt and pepper in a bowl; shape into tiny balls.
2 Heat water to boiling in a kettle; stir in onion soup mix; cover. Simmer 10 minutes.
3 Place meat balls in simmering soup; cover; simmer 15 minutes. Stir in tomatoes and beans and liquid; heat just to boiling; stir in parsley.
4 Ladle into soup bowls; serve with chowder crackers, if you wish.

Beef-Vegetable Potage
Ground meat, macaroni and three vegetables turn into a hearty supper in a hurry.
Makes 8 servings

1 pound ground beef
1 tablespoon vegetable oil

1 can (1 pound) diced carrots
1 can (1 pound) cut green beans
1 package (2 envelopes) cream of mushroom soup mix
2 cups diced celery
1 cup uncooked elbow macaroni
4 tablespoons instant minced onion
1 teaspoon salt
2 cups milk

1 Shape ground beef into a large patty; brown in vegetable oil in a heavy kettle 5 minutes on each side, then break up into chunks.
2 Drain liquids from carrots and green beans into an 8-cup measure; add enough water to make 8 cups. Stir into meat mixture, then stir in mushroom soup mix, celery, macaroni, onion and salt. Heat slowly, stirring constantly, to boiling, then cook, stirring often, 10 minutes.
3 Stir in carrots, beans and milk; heat slowly just until hot. Ladle into heated soup bowls.

Five-Star Soup
The five stars: Ham, sausages, macaroni, beans and vegetables. Big bowlfuls make a hearty main course.
Makes 8 servings

1 package (1 pound) dried large white navy beans
6 cups boiling water
1 shank end fully cooked or cook-before-eating ham (about 3 pounds)
4 cups shredded cabbage (about 1 pound)
2 cups thinly sliced pared carrots (about 7 medium-size)
1 large onion, chopped (1 cup)
1 cup chopped celery
1 clove garlic, minced
1 package (12 ounces) smoked sausage links, sliced thin
1 can (about 1 pound) tomatoes
1 teaspoon salt
½ teaspoon pepper
1 cup elbow macaroni (half an 8-ounce package)

1 Pick over beans, rinse and place in a large bowl. Pour the boiling water over; cover; let stand 1 hour.
2 Trim several small pieces of fat from ham; melt in a kettle or Dutch oven. Stir in cabbage, carrots, onion, celery and garlic; sauté slowly, stirring often, 20 minutes; remove and set aside for Step 4.
3 Pour beans and liquid into kettle; add ham, sliced sausages, tomatoes, salt, pepper and 6

cups more water. Heat to boiling; cover; simmer 1½ hours.

4 Remove ham from kettle. Cut meat from bone, trim off fat and dice meat. Stir into soup with vegetables from Step 2.

5 Cook 30 minutes, or until beans are tender; stir in macaroni. Continue cooking 15 minutes longer, or until macaroni is tender.

6 Ladle into a tureen or soup bowls; sprinkle with chopped parsley, if you wish.

Note: This soup tastes even better made a day ahead and reheated.

Minestrone

Zesty salami and plenty of vegetables and macaroni go into this Italian favorite.
Makes 8 servings

½ *pound (1 cup) dried white beans*
8 *cups water*
1 *pound salami, skinned and diced*
2 *cups chopped celery*
1 *can (about 1 pound) tomatoes*
1 *cup cubed pared yellow turnip*
¼ *cup chopped parsley*
1 *teaspoon leaf basil, crumbled*
4 *cups shredded cabbage*
2 *large zucchini, trimmed and sliced*
½ *cup elbow macaroni*
   Grated Parmesan cheese

1 Cover beans with 4 cups of the water in a large saucepan; heat to boiling; cover. Cook 2 minutes; remove from heat; let stand 1 hour.

2 Brown salami with celery in a kettle; stir in beans and liquid, tomatoes, turnip, parsley, basil and remaining 4 cups water; cover.

3 Heat slowly to boiling, then simmer 2 hours. Stir in cabbage and zucchini; simmer 30 minutes longer.

4 Heat soup to boiling; stir in macaroni. Cook 15 minutes longer, or until macaroni is tender.

5 Ladle into soup bowls; sprinkle with cheese.

Minute-Minded Minestrone

Makes 6 servings

½ *cup finely broken spaghetti*
1 *cup shredded cabbage*
1 *cup canned French-style green beans*
1 *clove of garlic, minced*
½ *teaspoon salt*
3 *cups boiling water*

Five-Star Soup, a medley of meat and vegetables.

1 *can (10¾ ounces) condensed minestrone soup*
1 *can (11½ ounces) condensed bean-and-bacon soup*
1 *can (10¾ ounces) condensed vegetable beef soup*
   Grated Parmesan cheese

1 Combine spaghetti, cabbage, green beans, garlic, salt and water in a kettle; cover. Simmer, stirring several times, 8 minutes.

2 Stir in soups; heat slowly just until bubbly. (Soup will be very thick. Add hot water, if needed, to prevent sticking.)

3 Ladle into bowls; sprinkle with cheese.

Vienna Sausage Chowder

Makes 6 servings

1 *medium-size onion, chopped (½ cup)*
2 *tablespoons butter or margarine*
1 *can (11¼ ounces) condensed split pea soup with ham*
1 *soup can of water*
1 *can (10¾ ounces) condensed vegetable soup*
1 *can (1 pound) tomatoes*
1 *teaspoon marjoram, crumbled*
½ *teaspoon salt*
⅛ *teaspoon garlic powder*
1 *can (4 ounces) Vienna sausages, drained and sliced*

1 Sauté onion in butter or margarine until soft in a large saucepan.

2 Stir in pea soup and water; heat, stirring constantly, to boiling. Stir in vegetable soup, tomatoes, marjoram, salt and garlic powder. Heat to boiling again; simmer 10 minutes.

3 Stir in Vienna sausages; heat just until sausages are hot. Ladle into heated soup bowls or plates. Serve with toasted sliced French bread.

Hotdog Hot Pot

Makes 6 servings

1 *pound frankfurters, sliced thin*
2 *tablespoons butter or margarine*
1 *large onion, diced (1 cup)*
2 *medium-size potatoes, pared and diced (2 cups)*
2 *large carrots, pared and sliced*
2 *cups water*

1865

SOUP KETTLE

1 teaspoon salt
1 teaspoon leaf thyme, crumbled
1 tablespoon Worcestershire sauce
1 large can (14½ ounces) evaporated milk
1 can (12 or 16 ounces) whole-kernel corn
1 tablespoon chopped parsley

1 Brown frankfurters lightly in butter or margarine in a heavy kettle; push to one side. Add
onion to kettle; sauté until soft.
2 Stir in potatoes, carrots, water, salt, thyme
and Worcestershire sauce. Heat to boiling;
cover.
3 Simmer 15 minutes, or until potatoes and
carrots are tender. Stir in evaporated milk and
corn; heat to boiling.
4 Ladle into a tureen or heated soup bowls;
sprinkle with parsley. Serve with chowder
crackers, if you wish.

●

Scandinavian Supper Pea Soup
This simple yet hearty soup tastes even better
made a day ahead and reheated.
Makes 8 servings

1 package (1 pound) dried split yellow peas
6 cups boiling water
½ pound lean salt pork
4 cups water
3 large carrots, pared and sliced
1 large leek, trimmed and sliced
1 large onion, chopped (1 cup)
½ teaspoon salt
¼ teaspoon leaf thyme, crumbled
⅛ teaspoon pepper
1 Kielbasa sausage, weighing about 1½
    pounds
  Chopped parsley
  Prepared mustard
  Dark pumpernickel

1 Place peas in a heavy kettle; pour in the 6
cups boiling water; cover. Let stand 1 hour. Heat
to boiling, then simmer, stirring often, 1½ hours.
Press through a sieve or food mill; return to
kettle and set aside for Step 3.
2 While peas cook, simmer salt pork in the 4
cups water in a large saucepan 1 hour; add
carrots, leek and onion. Cook 1 hour longer,
or until pork and vegetables are tender. Remove
pork to a cutting board; trim off rind; dice meat.
3 Stir vegetables with broth, pork, salt, thyme
and pepper into puréed peas in kettle; lay whole

1866

Scandinavian Supper Pea Soup, a golden blend.

sausage on top. Heat to boiling, then simmer 20 minutes, or until sausage is heated through.
4 Lift out sausage and place on a cutting board or platter.
5 Ladle soup into soup bowls; sprinkle with chopped parsley. Slice sausage to eat with mustard and bread along with the soup.

Country Pea Soup
Makes about 16 cups

    1 package (1 pound) split green peas
    8 cups water
    4 cups canned tomato juice
    1 ham bone or ham hock
1½ cups diced pared potato
    1 cup diced celery
    1 cup diced onion
    1 cup diced pared carrot
    1 bay leaf
    1 teaspoon salt
 ¼ teaspoon pepper
    1 cup ground cooked ham*
    1 egg
    2 tablespoons chopped parsley
    2 tablespoons all-purpose flour

1 Combine peas, water, tomato juice, ham bone or hock, potato, celery, onion, carrot, bay leaf, salt and pepper in large kettle; bring to boiling; lower heat and simmer, stirring occasionally, 1½ hours, or until peas are mushy-tender.
2 Remove ham bone or hock; cut off any lean meat to grind for ham balls (you will need 1 cup, so buy a meaty hock or use ham left over from a roast); combine ham with egg, parsley and flour; mix well.
3 Form meat mixture lightly into tiny balls (this amount makes about 28); drop into boiling soup about 10 minutes before serving time; simmer to heat through. Serve in big chowder bowls, as this soup is hearty food!

* Meat from bone or hock can be used for all or part of this.

1868

Herb Bread Chunks
Makes 8 servings

Halve 1 long loaf of French bread then split each half to make 4 pieces; slash pieces about 1 inch apart almost through to crusts. Spread generously with 1 stick (8 tablespoons) softened butter or margarine; sprinkle lightly with 2 tablespoons grated Parmesan cheese and ½ teaspoon mixed salad herbs. Place on cookie sheet; toast quickly in very hot oven (500°) 5 minutes, or until golden-crisp. Serve piping hot.

TWO DESSERT SOUPS

Fruit-Cup Soup
Chill this Scandinavian specialty for a few hours before mealtime to serve frosty-cold.
Makes 6 servings

    3 tablespoons quick-cooking tapioca
    2 tablespoons sugar
      Dash of salt
2½ cups water
    1 can (6 ounces) frozen concentrated orange juice
    2 peaches, peeled and sliced
    1 orange, peeled and sectioned
    1 banana, peeled and sliced
 ½ cup sliced hulled strawberries
      OR: ½ cup fresh raspberries or seedless grapes
    1 tablespoon lemon juice

1 Stir tapioca, sugar and salt into 1 cup water in small saucepan; heat to a full rolling boil, stirring constantly; pour into a medium-size bowl; stir in orange juice until melted; add remaining 1½ cups water; cool 15 minutes; stir; cover; chill.
2 Stir in prepared fruits and lemon juice (soup will be slightly thickened); serve in cups or dessert dishes.

Plum Chiller
Makes 8 servings

    2 pounds ripe red plums
 ¾ cup sugar
 ¼ teaspoon grated orange peel
    1 two-inch piece stick cinnamon
    4 cups water
    3 tablespoons quick-cooking tapioca

1 Wash plums; halve and pit. Combine with sugar, orange peel, cinnamon stick and water into a large saucepan. Heat to boiling, then simmer 20 minutes, or until plums are very soft; remove cinnamon stick.
2 Press mixture through a coarse sieve into a medium-size bowl; return to saucepan; stir in tapioca.
3 Heat, stirring constantly, to a full rolling boil, then simmer, stirring several times, 10 minutes, or until mixture thickens slightly. Pour into a medium-size bowl; cover. Chill several hours or overnight.
4 Ladle into cups or small dessert dishes; float a thin slice of orange on each serving, if you wish.

SOME OUT-OF-THE-CAN QUICKIES

Quick Tomato Bouillon—Heat 2½ cups canned tomato juice and 1 can (10½ ounces) condensed beef broth with 1 teaspoon crumbled leaf basil just to boiling; serve hot with a garnish of popcorn. Makes 4 servings.

Tomato Cream—Heat 2 cans (about 1 pound each) tomatoes, breaking up large pieces with a spoon. While tomatoes heat, sauté 1 chopped large onion in 4 tablespoons butter or margarine in large saucepan just until golden; remove from heat; stir in 4 tablespoons all-purpose flour, 1 teaspoon sugar, 1 teaspoon salt, ¼ teaspoon pepper and 2 cups milk. Cook, stirring constantly, until sauce thickens and boils 1 minute. Stir in heated tomatoes. Serve in heated mugs. Makes 6 servings.

Tomato-Gumbo Soup—Heat 1 can (10¾ ounces) condensed tomato soup and 1 can (10¾ ounces) condensed vegetable soup with 2 soup cans water, 1 bay leaf and ¼ teaspoon crumbled leaf oregano. Stir in ½ teaspoon filé powder, pour into bowls and top with a float of canned okra slices or, if you prefer, freshly grated Parmesan cheese. Makes 6 servings.

Mongole Soup—Combine in a medium-size saucepan 1 can (11¼ ounces) condensed green pea soup, 1 can (10¾ ounces) condensed tomato soup and 1 cup each milk and water. Heat but do not boil. Blend in dash of curry powder. Makes 4 servings.

Shrimp Mongole—Combine in a large saucepan 1 can (10¾ ounces) condensed tomato soup, 1 can (11¼ ounces) condensed green pea soup, 1 soup can water, ½ cup milk, 1 can (about 5 ounces) deveined shrimps, drained and cut crosswise, and ½ teaspoon each curry powder and grated lemon peel. Heat, stirring, until steamy-hot but do not boil. Serve topped with lemon slice. Makes 4 servings.

Quick Senegalese Soup—Combine in a medium-size saucepan 1 can (10½ ounces) condensed cream of chicken soup, 1 tall can (14½ ounces) evaporated milk, 1 tablespoon lemon juice and 1 teaspoon curry powder. Heat, stirring, until steamy-hot but do not boil. Serve hot or chill several hours and serve cold. Top, if you like, with toasted slivered almond. Makes 4 servings.

Double-Treat Cream Soup—In the top of a double boiler combine 1 can (10½ ounces) condensed cream of asparagus soup, 1 can (10½ ounces) condensed cream of mushroom soup, 1 soup can of water and 1 soup can of milk. Set over boiling water and heat, stirring often, 20 minutes. Serve in bowls with a few pretzel balls or sticks on top. Makes 6 servings.

Quick Cheddar Chowder—In a large saucepan combine 1 can (10¾ ounces) condensed vegetable soup, 1 can (10¾ ounces) condensed vegetarian-vegetable soup, 1 can (10¾ ounces) condensed Cheddar cheese soup, 2 soup cans water, 1 soup can milk and ¼ teaspoon seasoned pepper. Heat and stir just until mixture boils. Ladle into bowls and serve. Makes 6 servings.

Hash 'n Corn Soup—Mash 1 can (1 pound) corned beef hash in a saucepan; stir in 1 can (10¾ ounces) condensed tomato soup, 1 soup can water, 1 can (12 to 16 ounces) whole-kernel corn and liquid, ½ teaspoon Italian herb seasoning and 1 teaspoon Worcestershire sauce. Heat and stir until steamy-hot. Makes 6 servings.

All-American Soup—Sauté 1 chopped large onion in 2 tablespoons butter or margarine in a large saucepan; add ½ to 1 pound ground beef; cook slowly, breaking up meat with a fork. Stir in and heat 3½ cups water to boiling; add 1 envelope tomato-vegetable soup mix and 1 cup chopped celery and leaves; cover; boil 10 minutes. Stir in 1 can (about 1 pound) baked beans in tomato sauce and 1 cup canned tomato juice. Heat just to boiling and serve. Makes 8 servings.

Spanish Bean Soup—Stir 1 cup leftover mashed potatoes (or use ¼ cup packaged instant mashed potato) into 3 cups water in a large saucepan; add 1 can (about 20 ounces) chick peas and liquid; 1 can (8 ounces) tomato sauce; 1 grated carrot; 1 grated onion; 1 cup finely diced salami; 1 beef-bouillon cube; 1 teaspoon sugar and ¼ teaspoon crumbled leaf basil. Boil about 5 minutes to blend flavors; garnish with sliced stuffed olives and grated Parmesan cheese. Makes 8 servings

1869

Vichyssoise—In a medium-size saucepan combine 2 cans (10¼ ounces each) frozen cream of potato soup and 1 soup can each milk and light cream or table cream. Heat and stir over low heat until soup is thawed. Transfer, half at a time, to an electric-blender container and beat until creamy smooth. Chill at least 4 hours before serving. Makes 4 to 6 servings.

Hot off the grill, a sizzling steak crowned with butter-sautéed button mushrooms and served juicily rare.

STEAKS AND  CHOPS

STEAKS AND CHOPS:
BEEF, VEAL, LAMB, PORK AND HAM,
TIPS ON BUYING AND STORING,
RECIPES FOR LUXURY AND BUDGET
CUTS

America's favorite cuts of meat, if a poll could be taken, would no doubt be steaks and chops, with beefsteaks and pork chops topping the list.

There *are* steaks other than beefsteaks, of course, equally flavorsome and succulent, often far more economical. Lamb steaks, to name one, veal and ham steaks to name two others. As for chops, there are lamb chops—the shoulder cuts as well as the kingly rib and loin; there are also veal chops and cutlets.

Our purpose here is to include the whole luscious line of steaks and chops, the luxury-priced and the budget, showing the best ways of preparing each. And showing, too, how with skillful treatment, the less expensive steaks and chops, those often offered on "special" at your local supermarket, can be treated in much the same manner as the costly cuts with equally sensational results.

Included here, then, are dozens and dozens of recipes (all of them FAMILY CIRCLE favorites) for preparing your favorite steaks and chops as well as additional recipes for cooking some of the less familiar, money-saving cuts. There are also tips on buying and storing, tips on cooking indoors and out. A mini-cookbook, you might say, devoted entirely to steaks and chops: beef, veal, lamb, pork and ham.

* * *

TIPS ON BUYING STEAKS

Whether you cook them indoors or out, learn how to buy the best steak for the money and the occasion. The pointers here are worth remembering when you go shopping and the guide that follows will help you recognize the popular cuts.

The Big Luxury Three:
Porterhouse, sirloin and club steaks rank at the top, with T-bone a close runner-up, especially in twosome families. Supermarkets pride themselves on their excellent quality of beef, and for flavor and tenderness these steaks can't be beat. Buy them cut at least an inch thick, although it's amazing how an even thicker one has a juicier, meatier flavor. The easiest way to figure the amount you will need is to allow ½ pound each for average appetites, 1 pound for hearty ones.

The Budget Champs
The chuck-steak family takes the honors here. Blade chuck steak with its long flat bone,

round-bone chuck steak (its name describes it) and 7-bone arm chuck steak with a thin bone along one edge that looks like the numeral "7" are the leaders. In some areas of the country meatmen turn this popular cut into small steaks labeled with a special name such as "chicken steak," or "Mr. and Mrs. steak." Thanks to meat tenderizer, all can be broiled to perfection. And most steak fans will readily admit that chuck has *flavor!* Chuck is good to your budget too, and when it's on special, you win by stocking up. You can even buy one thick roast, bone it and split it into smaller steaks, or cut it up into meaty chunks for kebab cooking.

GALLERY OF POPULAR STEAKS

From grand porterhouse to humble sandwich steaks, your supermarket has a cut to suit your taste and your pocketbook. How many of these nine popular kinds do you know? Each promises steak value, steak goodness, and steak status whenever the call, "Let's have steak," goes up.

Porterhouse—Cut from the tenderest sirloin end, this de luxe steak is identified best by its T-shape bone and large tenderloin. A 1-inch cut—about 2 pounds—is generous for two.
Sirloin—Here's steak for a crowd; a 2-inch-thick cut, weighing 4 to 5 pounds, is enough for 6 to 8 servings. Sirloin costs less than porterhouse but rates high in steak flavor.
Round Steak—When cut full, steak is lean and oval in shape, with a small round bone. Meat cut just below the bone is top round; remaining, bottom. To broil, both should be tenderized.
T-Bone—The next cut to porterhouse, it is often called "small" porterhouse. It has the same T-bone, but a smaller tenderloin. A 1½-inch-thick slice will weigh from 1 to 2 pounds.
Rib Steak—This choice, with all of the same good flavor of a rib roast, comes either boned or unboned. A one-serving steak cut an inch thick will weigh about 10 ounces to 1 pound.
Flank Steak—It's flat and thin with no bones or fat, and is seldom featured because there are only two to each animal. Buy top quality, then broil fast—3 to 4 minutes on a side.
Club—An individual steak, sometimes called Delmonico. It has no tenderloin, but otherwise is the same as porterhouse and T-bone. One steak an inch thick will weigh 10 to 16 ounces.
Chuck Steak—Cut from the shoulder with a long-blade, round or 7-shape bone, this steak

1872

Braised veal chops served on a bed of sweet green peas.

A hefty chuck steak, if marinated with meat tenderizer, can be broiled like sirloin. It's tasty budget fare.

is a thrifty buy. To broil, use tenderizer. Or simmer it in seasoned sauce, Swiss-steak style. **Sandwich Steaks**—Often called cube, minute or quick. They are boneless, and flattened by a mechanical cutter. All are thrifty choices to tenderize, if you wish, then pan-fry fast.

TIPS ON STORING STEAKS:

• Loosen the wrapper on packaged meat to let air circulate around it, then place it in the meat compartment or coldest part of your refrigerator. Or to save last-minute work, unwrap meat and trim as needed, then wrap loosely in wax paper and store.
• For best eating, plan to cook steak within three days.
• To freeze, trim the meat, then rewrap tightly in freezer paper, label, date and freeze.

TIPS ON COOKING STEAKS:

• All steaks under one inch are best pan-broiled. Heat a heavy frying pan sizzling-hot and grease lightly, if you wish, or sprinkle pan lightly with salt. Brown the steak quickly, turning just once. Moisture starting to appear on top is your cue for turning.

• For broiling, choose steak at least an inch thick, trim some fat so drippings won't flare up, then slash fat edge so meat won't curl. Grease broiler rack with fat trimmings before starting. Use tongs or a fork stuck into fat edge for turning, and salt the meat *after* turning, rather than before, as salt tends to draw out the meat juices.

• Figure your cooking time carefully. And remember that steaks cooked rare to medium will be the juiciest.

INDOOR-OUTDOOR STEAK COOKING TIMETABLE*

Approximate Minutes per Side

Thickness of Steak	1 inch	1½ inches	2 inches
Grill Outdoors			
Rare	8 to 10	12 to 14	14 to 16
Medium	12 to 14	16 to 18	18 to 20
Broil Indoors			
Rare	6	9	16
Medium	7	10	20

*Use the time table as a *guide* only, as actual time depends on the temperature of the meat, how hot the fire is and the distance of the meat from the fire. *To Test for Doneness:* Cut a small slit near the bone or near the center if the steak is boneless.

TIPS ON BUYING CHOPS

The many kinds and cuts of chops—from double-thick for stuffing to extra-thin for pan-frying—offer wide mealtime possibilities. Learn the differences among all types in pork, lamb and veal, what they cost and how to cook them, and you'll come out ahead at the check-out counter and in eating enjoyment.

Why Prices Differ

There's more to an animal than chops. For example, from a pig weighing 210 pounds, only seven pounds will show up as center-cut pork chops. Because the supply is limited and many shoppers want them, the price per pound is naturally higher than for more plentiful, less popular choices. But a store must sell all of its fresh meat, so to attract buyers it sets a lower price on slower-moving cuts. Get the most for your money by considering all prices and cuts in terms of your meal plans. As an example: Shoulder veal or lamb chops or end-cut pork chops will be the thriftiest of all, yet they will fit just as smoothly into everyday menus as the higher-price cuts do, without shortchanging either good eating or good health. Another reminder: Because shoulder chops are often on special, you'll save even more.

The Popular Chops

From place to place, or even from store to store, names of chops vary. That's why the shape of the bone—the same for veal, pork and lamb—is a good clue to identification, tenderness and cooking style. For the four leading kinds of chops, here are the facts:

Loin—Sometimes called tenderloin or center-cut loin chops. These are easily recognized by their T-shape bone that corresponds to the one in porterhouse and T-bone beefsteaks. Each has a generous "eye" of lean meat with some tenderloin.

Rib—Also sometimes tagged center-cut rib chops. They contain a part of the rib and backbone. Although they have a "rib eye" that's the meaty part, there is no tenderloin.

Sirloin—In lamb or pork, some stores call these steaks. Each has a wedge or round bone with more lean in comparison to bone than any other type of chop.

Shoulder—You'll find two kinds: Arm and blade chops. Arm chops have a small round bone; blade chops, a long thin bone. Both are economical, but blade will usually cost less.

Some Specialty Chops

These are other definitions worth knowing. Because of regional preferences, you won't find all of the cuts in every supermarket—or every time you go shopping.

Frenched—Usually cut from lamb, but you may also see pork sold this way. Meat is stripped from the end of a rib or loin chop; then a paper frill is slipped over the bone end.

Kidney—Look for lamb or veal, each with a slice of kidney.

Butterfly—A real mealtime treat, these chops start as a double-thick slice of pork loin. The slice is slit partway through the center, then opened into a butterfly shape.

Saratoga—Rolled lamb shoulder makes this boneless chop.

English—A gourmet's delight, this double-thick loin lamb chop is boned and fastened to give it its chunky round shape. It contains both loin and tenderloin.

Smoked—Cut from a pork loin (just as fresh chops are), then cured and smoked for a mild

Rib pork chops, if cut very thick, can be stuffed with a variety of stuffings. Cut a pocket deep in each chop, then fill with your favorite stuffing mixture or, if you prefer, with diced or chopped fruits or vegetables.

homelike flavor. They come both bone-in and boneless, and most are fully cooked, so be sure to check the label for fixing directions.

How Much to Buy
It's a snap to get just enough for one meal, as you can see how much meat is on each chop. Or count noses and allow two thin or one thick chop per person for dinner. Stated another way, one pound for two servings is a good rule of thumb.

TIPS ON STORING CHOPS

Like all fresh meat, chops need special treatment to be at their flavorful best. If you plan to use them within a day or two, just place the store package in the refrigerator without breaking the seal. Have a few extra minutes? Get them ready for cooking this way: Trim off any excess fat, then place the chops on a tray, cover loosely with wax paper or transparent wrap to allow the air to circulate around them, and chill. For storage beyond two to three days and up to about three months, look to your freezer.

TIPS ON COOKING CHOPS

Generally speaking, these favorites can be broiled, pan-broiled, pan-fried, grilled, braised or baked. However, it's good to remember these few basic rules:

Pan-fry or pan-broil pork or lamb chops that are less than an inch thick to keep them moist and juicy.

Braise all shoulder chops. This means to brown them first in a frying pan, then cook slowly, covered, until tender in a small amount of liquid. Flavorful choices: Bouillon, fruit juice, tomato-juice cocktail or soup.

Cook pork chops well done, however you fix them. When broiled or grilled outdoors, keep the heat low so the meat will be cooked through to the center (no traces of pink) by the time the outside is browned. To test for doneness, cut a small slit in the center of the chop near the end of the cooking time.

Pan-fry, bake or braise veal chops until well done to bring out their delicate flavor and juiciness. Because veal is lean, broiling only toughens and dries the meat. Bread pork or veal chops, then chill the chops after adding the coating. This helps it to stick to the meat—not to the pan—during cooking.

1875

BEEF

Steak on a Stick
Makes 6 servings

12 small potatoes, unpared
12 small onions, unpeeled
 6 medium-size carrots, pared and cut in 2-inch
    pieces
 2 pounds zucchini squash, cut in 1-inch
    pieces
 2 pounds top round or sirloin steak, cut in
    2-inch cubes
    Vegetable oil for brushing
    ZIPPY TOMATO SAUCE (recipe follows)

1 Thread potatoes, onions, carrots and zucchini on separate large greased skewers. (Vegetables take longer to cook than meat, so start them first.) Brush potatoes and onions with vegetable oil; carrots and zucchini with ZIPPY TOMATO SAUCE.
2 Place on grill over glowing coals; cook, turning often and basting with oil or sauce, until tender. Onions and carrots take about 45 minutes, potatoes and zucchini about 30 minutes.
3 While vegetables cook, thread steak cubes on large greased skewers. (Meat will cook more evenly if not crowded.) Brush with sauce; grill along with vegetables, basting once or twice with sauce, 5 to 10 minutes, or until done as you like steak.
    ZIPPY TOMATO SAUCE—Sauté 1 chopped onion and 1 minced clove of garlic in 2 tablespoons olive oil 5 minutes; stir in 2 tablespoons brown sugar, 1 teaspoon prepared mustard, 1 teaspoon chili powder, 1 teaspoon salt, 1 can (8 ounces) tomato sauce, 1 cup water, ¼ cup cider vinegar and 1 tablespoon Worcestershire sauce; simmer about 1 hour. Makes about 1½ cups.

Broiled Boneless Steak
The secret of its rich brown crust and tender juiciness is its spicy dry marinade.
Makes 6 servings

 1 piece round or boneless chuck steak, cut
    1½ inches thick (about 3 pounds)
1½ teaspoons unseasoned meat tenderizer
 1 teaspoon garlic powder
 1 teaspoon dry mustard

1 Remove steak from refrigerator ½ hour before cooking; place in shallow pan.

Steak Madrid and Tournedos with Mushrooms Royale.

2 Combine remaining ingredients in a small cup; sprinkle evenly on both sides of steak. Pierce steak deeply all over with a fork; cover lightly with wax paper and let stand at room temperature, following time given on meat-tenderizer label.
3 Place on grill on rack set about 6 inches above hot coals; grill, turning once or twice, until outside is richly browned and meat is done as you like it. Time will depend on heat of coals and distance of meat from fire bed, but it should average at least 15 minutes on each side for rare.
4 To serve, place steak on carving board and cut diagonally into ½-inch-thick slices.

Steak Madrid
Broil your choice of steaks to slice and serve with a dressy herb sauce.
Makes 6 servings

 1 sirloin, chuck or round beef steak, cut about
    1½ inches thick
 ½ cup stuffed small Spanish olives (from an
    about-5-ounce jar)
 2 tablespoons prepared mustard
 2 tablespoons bottled steak sauce
    BUTTERED ONION RINGS (recipe follows)
    SAUCE CONTINENTAL (recipe follows)

1 Remove steak from refrigerator 1 hour before cooking. (If using chuck or round steak, moisten meat and sprinkle with instant unseasoned meat tenderizer, following label directions.) Make cuts, about 3 inches deep and 1 inch apart, into steak all around edge with a sharp knife; push olives deep into cuts.
2 Place steak on rack in broiler pan. Combine mustard and steak sauce in a cup; brush part evenly over top of steak.
3 Broil, following range manufacturer's directions, 9 minutes for rare or 10 minutes for medium; turn. Brush with remaining mustard mixture. Broil about 9 minutes longer, or until steak is done as you like it.
4 Remove to a cutting board; top with BUTTERED ONION RINGS; garnish with cherry tomatoes and parsley, if you wish. Slice steak and serve with SAUCE CONTINENTAL.
    BUTTERED ONION RINGS—Peel 1 medium-size yellow onion; slice and separate into rings. Sauté in 2 tablespoons butter or margarine just until soft in a small frying pan.

Sauce Continental
Fluffy and richly seasoned—and a perfect crown for your special steak.
Makes about 1 cup

1877

Carioca Pepper Steaks are a Latin interpretation of the classic Steak au Poivre. The pepper is a blend.

½ cup apple juice
1 tablespoon finely chopped onion
1 tablespoon cider vinegar
1 teaspoon leaf tarragon, crumbled
2 egg yolks
½ cup (1 stick) butter or margarine, melted
  Dash of cayenne
1 teaspoon chopped parsley

1 Combine apple juice, onion, vinegar and tarragon in a small saucepan. Heat to boiling, then simmer, uncovered, 10 minutes, or until mixture measures about ⅓ cup. Strain into a cup for Step 3.
2 Beat egg yolks slightly in top of a small double boiler; stir in about ⅓ cup of the melted butter or margarine. Place over simmering, *not boiling*, water.
3 Beat in strained liquid, alternately with remaining melted butter or margarine, with an electric or rotary beater; continue beating, keeping over simmering water, until mixture is fluffy-thick. Remove from heat at once.
4 Stir in cayenne and chopped parsley. Serve warm.

Carioca Pepper Steaks
Spunky seasoning is bright-hued pepper blend. Your broiler does the rest.
Makes 4 servings

2 boneless rump or round steaks, cut 1 inch
  thick
  Unseasoned instant meat tenderizer
2 tablespoons bottled steak sauce
2 teaspoons seasoned pepper
1 can (3½ ounces) French-fried onion rings

1 Moisten steaks and sprinkle with meat tenderizer, following label directions. Brush one side of each steak with steak sauce, then sprinkle with half of the seasoned pepper.
2 Broil 4 to 6 inches from heat 7 to 8 minutes for rare, 9 to 10 minutes for medium. Turn; brush with remaining steak sauce and sprinkle evenly with remaining seasoned pepper. Broil 7 to 10 minutes longer, or until done as you like steak.
3 While steaks broil, heat onion rings in pie plate in oven. Place steaks on cutting board; slice thin on the diagonal; garnish with onion rings.

Pepper Steak Broil
It's hot and peppery—just the way pepper steak fans like it!
Makes 6 servings

Pepper Steak Broil is aromatic of garlic and herbs.

STEAKS AND CHOPS

1 slice round steak, cut 1 inch thick (about
   2 pounds)
   Instant unseasoned meat tenderizer
1¼ cups wine vinegar or cider vinegar
½ cup olive oil or vegetable oil
1 tablespoon mixed Italian herbs
2 cloves of garlic, minced
1 bay leaf
1 tablespoon seasoned pepper

1 Moisten steak and sprinkle with meat tenderizer, following label directions. Place in a shallow glass or plastic dish.
2 Mix wine vinegar or cider vinegar, olive oil
or vegetable oil, herbs, garlic and bay leaf in
a 2-cup measure; pour over meat; cover. Chill
about 2 hours, turning meat several times so
it will season evenly.
3 When ready to broil, remove steak from
marinade. (Save marinade to strain, heat and
use as a dip or sauce for steak, if you wish.)
Place steak on broiler rack; sprinkle top evenly
with half of the seasoned pepper.
4 Broil, about 6 inches from heat, 10 to 12
minutes; turn; sprinkle with remaining seasoned
pepper. Broil 8 to 10 minutes longer for rare,
or until steak is done as you like it.
5 Remove to a cutting board; cut diagonally into

¼- to ½-inch-thick slices. Serve with skillet-
browned potatoes, if you wish.

Steak Special Broiler Meal
Handy instant marinade tenderizes and flavors
this steak.
Makes 4 servings

1 bone-in chuck steak (about 2 pounds)
1 envelope (about 1 ounce) instant meat
   marinade
1 can (10½ ounces) condensed beef broth
1 can (1 pound) whole tomatoes
   Bottled Italian salad dressing
½ cup water
2 tablespoons wine vinegar
3 tablespoons all-purpose flour

1 Trim any excess fat from steak and score
remaining fat edge every inch. Combine instant
meat marinade with ⅔ cup of the beef broth
in a shallow dish. Place steak in dish and turn
several times to coat evenly with marinade.
Marinate 15 minutes, piercing steak with a two-
tined fork, following marinade label directions.
2 Remove steak from marinade and pat dry with
paper toweling; reserve marinade for Step 4.

When broiling a steak, either on the outdoor grill or in the oven, snip the fatty edge so steak lies flat.

A juicy broiled steak with all the classic accompaniments: the crispest green salad, French bread chunks.

3 Broil steak 4 inches from heat for 6 minutes; turn. Add drained tomatoes; brush with salad dressing. Broil 6 minutes longer, or until steak is done.
4 Combine reserved meat marinade, remaining beef broth, water, vinegar and flour in a small saucepan. Heat, stirring constantly, until mixture thickens and boils 1 minute. Serve separately.

Barbecued Steak-Roast
Seasoned with peppery bottled sauce, this thick cut grills crusty-brown outside, juicy-tender inside.
Makes 6 servings

  1 round- or blade-bone chuck steak or boneless round steak, cut about 1½ inches thick (about 2½ pounds)
    Instant unseasoned meat tenderizer
½ cup bottled barbecue sauce

1 Trim excess fat from steak, leaving a narrow strip around edge, then score about every inch so meat will lie flat during cooking.

2 Sprinkle steak with tenderizer, following label directions; brush with sauce.
3 Grill over hot coals 15 minutes; turn; brush again with barbecue sauce. Grill 15 minutes longer for rare, or until done as you like it. (Time will depend on how hot coals are and distance of meat from them.)
4 Remove to cutting board; carve meat diagonally into about-½-inch-thick slices.

Barbecued Steak Special
Here's easy cheffing! Jumbo steak seasons in a spicy marinade before grilling.
Makes 6 servings

  1 round- or blade-bone chuck steak, cut about 1½ inches thick (about 3 pounds)
½ cup bottled spicy-tomato French dressing
    Instant unseasoned meat tenderizer
    CHIVES BUTTER *(recipe follows)*

1 Trim fat edge of steak; marinate steak in French dressing 1 hour before grilling.
2 When ready to cook, remove steak and sprinkle with meat tenderizer, following label

1881

Anchovy Steak wears an olive and anchovy lattice trim.

directions. Grill over hot coals 15 minutes; turn; grill 15 minutes longer for rare, or until meat is done as you like it. (Time will depend on how hot coals are and distance of meat from them.)

3 Top steak with CHIVES BUTTER; cut around bone, then carve meat diagonally into ½-inch-thick slices.

CHIVES BUTTER—Cut 1 stick (¼ pound) butter or margarine into 12 pats; pile into bowl; sprinkle with 2 tablespoons cut chives. Makes 6 servings, 2 pats each.

Anchovy Steak
Makes 4 servings

1 *blade-bone chuck beefsteak, weighing about 2½ pounds*
Instant meat tenderizer
2 *tablespoons all-purpose flour*
Vegetable oil
1 *can (2 ounces) flat anchovy fillets, drained*
Sliced pimiento-stuffed olives

1 Trim any excess fat from steak. Moisten meat; sprinkle with meat tenderizer, following label directions. Place on rack in broiler pan.
2 Sprinkle top of steak with 1 tablespoon of the flour; brush lightly with oil.
3 Broil, 3 to 4 inches from heat, 3 to 4 minutes for rare, or 5 to 6 minutes for medium; turn. Sprinkle remaining 1 tablespoon flour over top; brush with oil.
4 Continue broiling 2 to 3 minutes for rare, or 3 to 4 minutes for medium; remove from broiler.
5 Arrange anchovies in a pattern of squares on steak; place an olive slice in each square; brush all lightly with oil. Broil 2 to 3 minutes longer, or until steak is as done as you like it. Remove to a heated serving platter. Garnish platter with tomato roses and watercress and serve with French fried potatoes, if you wish. (To make a tomato rose, cut a medium-size tomato, from blossom end to within ¼ inch of bottom, into 8 wedges. Peel skin back slightly from points at top; center with a tiny sprig of parsley.)

Budget Steak Broil
Chunky cut of lean beef seasons in a zippy tomato-garlic dressing before it goes into the broiler.
Makes 6 servings

3 *pounds chuck steak, cut about 1½ inches thick*
½ *cup bottled tomato-garlic French dressing*
Instant unseasoned meat tenderizer

1 Brush both sides of steak with French dressing; place steak in shallow glass or plastic dish; let stand at room temperature 1 hour before cooking.

2 When ready to broil steak, score fat edges, then sprinkle with tenderizer, following label directions. Place on broiler rack.

3 Broil, following range manufacturer's directions, or about 12 to 14 minutes on each side for rare, 16 to 18 minutes for medium, or until done as you like steak.

4 Place steak on cutting board; cut around bone; carve meat diagonally into ½-inch-thick slices.

Santa Rosa Steak

Start with boneless chuck or round—both budget-smart cuts, as they're all meat.
Makes 6 servings

1 can (10½ ounces) condensed beef bouillon
1 can (8 ounces) tomato sauce
¼ cup olive oil or vegetable oil
2 tablespoons lemon juice
1 tablespoon minced onion
1 teaspoon salt
1 teaspoon sugar
1 teaspoon leaf basil, crumbled
1 teaspoon paprika
2½ pounds boneless chuck or round steak, cut
    1½ inches thick
    Instant unseasoned meat tenderizer

1 Combine beef bouillon, tomato sauce, olive oil or vegetable oil, lemon juice, onion, salt, sugar, basil and paprika in small saucepan; simmer 10 minutes to blend flavors; cool.

2 Moisten steak and sprinkle with meat tenderizer, following label directions. Place in a shallow glass or plastic dish; pour cooled marinade over. Cover; chill several hours, or overnight.

3 When ready to grill, lift steak from marinade with fork, letting excess liquid drain back. Place on grill about 6 inches above hot coals.

4 Grill, basting with marinade, 10 to 15 minutes for rare. (Time will depend on how hot coals

The best way to carve a giant broiled steak is across the grain, slightly on the bias and very, very thin.

STEAKS AND CHOPS

are.) Turn; baste again and grill 10 minutes longer, or until done as you like steak.

5 Place on carving board; cut diagonally into ½-inch-thick slices; heat any remaining marinade and spoon over.

Oven-Baked Cheddar Steak

Ribbons of melty cheese and crunchy pecans crown a family-size steak that "grills" to your taste without turning.
Bake at 450° for 25 minutes. Makes 6 servings

> 1 chuck beef steak, weighing about 3½ pounds
>   Instant unseasoned meat tenderizer
> 3 tablespoons bottled steak sauce
> ¼ cup chopped pecans
> ½ cup grated Cheddar cheese

1 Remove steak from refrigerator 1 hour before cooking. When ready to cook, sprinkle with meat tenderizer, following label directions; brush both sides with steak sauce; place on rack in broiler pan.

2 Bake in very hot oven (450°) 25 minutes for rare, or until done as you like steak; remove from oven; turn off heat.

3 Sprinkle pecans, then cheese over steak; return to heated oven just until cheese melts.

4 Carve into ¼-inch-thick slices; spoon juices over. Serve with SKILLET PEPPER RINGS (recipe follows), if you wish.

Skillet Pepper Rings

A colorful vegetable go-with for steak—or any other meat.
Makes 6 servings

Cut 2 medium-size sweet green peppers and 2 medium-size sweet red peppers crosswise into 6 thick slices each; remove seeds and membrane. Place rings in a medium-size frying pan; cover with boiling water; cover. Let stand 3 minutes, then drain. Add 4 tablespoons (½ stick) butter or margarine; sprinkle with ½ teaspoon salt; cover. Simmer, stirring once or twice, 10 minutes, or until tender.

"Tournedos" Henri IV

A gourmet specialty with a budget price, when you make your own "tournedos" from bone-in chuck roast.
This is a two-part recipe. You need one bone-in chuck roast, 2 inches thick and weighing about 3 pounds. Divide into two sections (see sketch). "Tournedos" are made from the tender section. Save the less tender section for making stew or pot roast. For easier cutting of raw beef, partially freeze 1 hour to firm meat.
Makes 4 servings

> Tender section from bone-in chuck roast (about 1¼ pounds)
> ¼ cup dry white wine

Here's a unique steak recipe—Oven-Baked Cheddar Steak accompanied by colorful Skillet Pepper Rings.

True tournedos are cut from the fillet but "Tournedos" Henri IV come from the much cheaper chuck.

 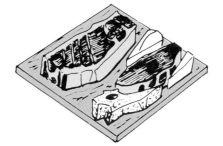 

1 teaspoon leaf tarragon, crumbled
1 teaspoon instant minced onion
1 envelope hollandaise-sauce mix
4 toast rounds, 4 inches in diameter
1 can (10 ounces) artichoke hearts

1 With sharp knife divide meat into tender section and less tender (see sketch) and discard bone. Reserve less tender section for stew or pot roast.

2 Cut the tender section in half, crosswise. Tie string an inch from each end of each piece. (This shapes pieces into compact rounds.) Cut between strings to make 2 individual "tournedos" from each piece.

3 Simmer wine, tarragon and onion for 5 minutes in a small saucepan; remove from heat; strain into a 1-cup measure. Prepare hollandaise-sauce mix, following label directions; gradually add strained herb-flavored wine, beating constantly. Keep warm.

4 Broil "tournedos" 4 inches from heat, 4 minutes; turn; broil 4 minutes longer, or until steaks are as done as you like them.

5 Meanwhile, heat, drain and season artichoke hearts.

6 Arrange toast rounds on heated platter. Top each with a "tournedo;" place one artichoke heart on each; spoon part of the sauce over each. Garnish with watercress and cherry tomatoes, if you wish. Serve remaining artichoke hearts and sauce separately.

Tournedos with Mushrooms Royale
Although party-fancy, this platter takes very little time from frying pan to table.
Makes 6 servings

MUSHROOMS ROYALE (recipe follows)
6 individual boneless chuck or club beef steaks, cut ¾ inch thick
Instant unseasoned meat tenderizer
4 tablespoons (½ stick) butter or margarine
⅛ teaspoon seasoned salt
⅛ teaspoon paprika
6 bread rounds, toasted and buttered

1 Make MUSHROOMS ROYALE.

2 Moisten chuck steaks and sprinkle with meat tenderizer, following label directions. (No need to tenderize club steaks.)

3 Brown quickly on each side in a sizzling-hot large heavy frying pan; remove; lower heat to medium. Melt butter or margarine in same pan; return steaks; sprinkle with seasoned salt and paprika. Pan-fry 3 to 4 minutes on each side for medium, or until steaks are done as you like them.

4 Arrange toast rounds on a heated serving platter; place a steak on each; spoon drippings from pan over steaks. Top with MUSHROOMS ROYALE. Garnish platter with watercress and serve with seasoned hot mashed potatoes, if you wish.

1886

Mushrooms Royale
Each delicate mushroom cap holds a rich pâté filling.
Makes 6 servings

6 large fresh mushrooms
1 tablespoon butter or margarine
2 teaspoons lemon juice
1 can (4¾ ounces) liver spread
1 tablespoon light cream or table cream
    1 pimiento, cut into thin strips

1 Wash mushrooms; cut off stems close to caps; dry caps on paper toweling. Chop stems fine.

2 Melt butter or margarine in a small frying pan; stir in lemon juice. Add mushroom caps and sauté, turning several times, 2 to 3 minutes, or just until heated through; remove with a slotted spoon.

3 Sauté chopped stems lightly in same pan; stir into liver spread in a small bowl; blend in cream until smooth.

4 Stuff into mushroom caps, dividing evenly. Garnish with pimiento strips.

Parslied Steaks
Makes 4 to 6 servings

6 frozen chopped beef steaks (from a 2-pound package)
4 tablespoons butter or margarine
4 green onions, trimmed and chopped
½ cup chopped parsley
½ teaspoon salt
½ teaspoon leaf marjoram, crumbled
¼ teaspoon cracked or coarse grind pepper

1 Sauté steaks on both sides, following label directions, in butter or margarine in a large skillet; remove to hot platter, overlapping steaks; keep warm while making sauce.

2 Sauté green onions in drippings in skillet until soft; stir in parsley, salt, marjoram and pepper; heat just until bubbling. Pour down center of steaks. Frame with broccoli spears and pan-browned potatoes, if you wish.

Beef Scaloppine
This dish is made from very thin slices of bottom round beef roast.
Makes 6 servings

12 thin slices from a bottom round beef roast
1 egg
2 tablespoons water
½ cup unsifted all-purpose flour
1 teaspoon salt
¼ teaspoon pepper
2 tablespoons butter or margarine
2 tablespoons vegetable oil
½ cup dry white wine
1 can (3 or 4 ounces) sliced mushrooms

When cut extra thick, broiled extra rare and carved extra thin, a steak might pass for prime rib roast.

1887

All steaks aren't priced out of sight. These frozen chopped beef steaks, served as Parslied Steaks, are princely fare available at a pauper's share.

1 Pound beef slices with a wooden or metal meat mallet until slices are very thin.

2 Beat egg and water until blended in a pie plate. Combine flour, salt and pepper in a shallow dish. Dip beef slices, first into beaten egg, then into seasoned flour.

3 Heat butter or margarine and oil in a large skillet. Brown beef slices, a few at a time, turning once, 2 minutes on each side. Remove to a hot platter and keep warm.

4 Stir wine and sliced mushrooms with their liquid into skillet. Cook, stirring constantly, scraping to loosen cooked-on juices in skillet. Boil 1 minute to reduce volume. Pour over beef on platter. Garnish with chopped parsley, if you wish.

Minute Steaks Monaco
Combine steak with vegetables and flavorful sauce to tempt the palate.
Makes 4 servings

- 4 minute steaks, about 6 ounces each
- 1 teaspoon salt
- 2 tablespoons vegetable oil
- 1 small eggplant, cut into ½-inch slices and pared
- 1 can (10½ ounces) condensed chicken broth
- 1 can (8 ounces) tomato sauce with mushrooms
- ½ teaspoon leaf oregano, crumbled
- 2 tablespoons all-purpose flour
- ¼ cup water
- Pitted ripe olives

1 Cook steaks in a very hot skillet that has been sprinkled with salt, 3 minutes on each side for rare. Remove from skillet and keep warm on heated serving platter.

2 Add oil to skillet. Brown eggplant slices on each side in hot oil. Stir in chicken broth, tomato sauce and oregano. Cover skillet and simmer 5 minutes, or until eggplant is tender.

3 Make a smooth paste of flour and water in a cup; stir into bubbling liquid in skillet; cook, stirring constantly, until mixture thickens and boils 1 minute.

4 Arrange eggplant slices under steaks in serving platter and top with sauce. Garnish with olives.

1888

Red and Green Pepper Beef
Makes 6 servings

- 2 medium-size green peppers, halved, seeded and thinly sliced
- 2 medium-size sweet red peppers, halved, seeded and thinly sliced

- 2 tablespoons olive oil or vegetable oil
- 1 chuck steak fillet (about 1½ pounds)
- 1 cup water
- 1 teaspoon Italian seasoning, crumbled
- 1 teaspoon salt
- ¼ teaspoon pepper

1 Sauté peppers in oil until soft in large skillet; remove to hot platter; keep warm.

2 Cook steak in oil remaining in skillet, turning once, 5 minutes on each side or until steak is as done as you like it. Slice steak and arrange with peppers on hot platter.

3 Stir water, Italian seasoning, salt and pepper into skillet. Cook, stirring constantly, scraping to loosen cooked-on juices in skillet. Boil 3 minutes to reduce volume by one-third. Pour over sliced beef and peppers. Serve with hot cooked rice, if you wish.

Chicken Steakettes
Home-style eating at its best in many parts of the country. Steak is "breaded," sautéed, then served with creamy gravy.
Makes 6 servings

- 1 slice round steak, cut 1 inch thick (about 2 pounds)
  Instant unseasoned meat tenderizer
- 1 small can evaporated milk (⅔ cup)
- 1 teaspoon salt
- ¼ teaspoon pepper
- ½ cup unsifted all-purpose flour
- 4 tablespoons (½ stick) butter or margarine
  CREAM STEAK GRAVY (recipe follows)

1 Moisten steak and sprinkle with meat tenderizer, following label directions; cut diagonally into ¼-inch-thick slices with a sharp knife.

2 Combine evaporated milk, salt and pepper in a pie plate; measure flour onto wax paper. Dip steak slices into milk mixture, then into flour to coat both sides well.

3 Sauté, a few slices at a time, in butter or margarine in a large frying pan 4 minutes on each side, or until richly browned.

4 Place on heated serving platter; keep hot while cooking remaining meat and making CREAM STEAK GRAVY.

CREAM STEAK GRAVY—Tip frying pan and let fat rise in one corner; pour off all fat into a cup. Return 4 tablespoons fat to pan; blend in 4 tablespoons flour; cook, stirring all the time, just until mixture bubbles. Stir in 1 cup milk and 1 cup water slowly; continue cooking and stir-

Another bargain steak with big appeal: Steak Slices with Onion-Butter Balls. The steak used is flank.

ring, scraping any cooked-on juices from bottom and side of pan, until gravy thickens and boils 1 minute. Season to taste with salt and pepper. Makes 2 cups.

Sliced London Broil
Makes 4 servings

Buy 1 choice-grade flank steak weighing about 1½ pounds. Place on broiler rack; brush lightly with bottled thick meat sauce; broil, with top of meat 3 inches from heat, 3 minutes; turn; brush again with meat sauce; broil 3 to 4 minutes longer, or until done as you like it. Cut diagonally across the grain into thin slices; serve on a plank or ovenproof platter with mashed potatoes browned lightly in broiler while you are slicing steak.

Steak Slices with Onion-Butter Balls
Little blobs of onion-seasoned butter melt atop speedy-broiled steak.
Makes 6 servings

1 flank steak (about 2 pounds)
  Instant unseasoned meat tenderizer
  Salt and pepper
4 tablespoons (½ stick) butter or margarine
  Instant minced onion

1 Moisten steak and sprinkle with meat tenderizer, following label directions.
2 Broil, following range manufacturer's directions, 3 to 4 minutes on each side for rare, 5 to 6 minutes for medium, or until done as you like steak. Season with salt and pepper.
3 While steak broils, shape butter or margarine into 6 balls; roll in onion.
4 Remove steak to cutting board; carve diagonally into thin slices; place on heated serving plates or platter. Top each serving with a butter ball.

1889

Oriental Steak Broil
Tender lean flank seasons in a soy-sparked sauce before broiling.
Makes 6 servings

STEAKS AND CHOPS

1 flank steak, weighing about 1½ pounds
3 tablespoons lemon juice
1 tablespoon soy sauce
1 clove garlic, minced
1½ teaspoons salt
¼ teaspoon aniseed, crushed
⅛ teaspoon pepper

1 Pierce steak all over with a fork; place in a shallow pan.
2 Combine lemon juice, soy sauce, garlic, salt, aniseed and pepper in a cup; pour over steak. Chill, turning steak several times, 3 to 4 hours to season.
3 When ready to broil, remove steak from marinade; place on rack in broiler pan.
4 Broil, following range manufacturer's directions, 3 to 4 minutes; turn. Brush with marinade. Broil 3 to 4 minutes longer for rare, or until steak is done as you like it.
5 Place on a cutting board; carve diagonally into ½-inch-thick slices.

Gourmet Steak Platter
What a morale booster! Steak is brushed with zippy salad dressing, broiled, sliced and served with a hidden cabbage surprise.
Makes 6 servings

½ head of cabbage (about 1½ pounds)
1½ teaspoons salt
¾ teaspoon caraway seeds
1 flank steak (about 2 pounds)
  Instant unseasoned meat tenderizer
4 tablespoons Italian salad dressing
  Parsley

1 Place cabbage in a medium-size saucepan with salt, caraway seeds and enough water almost to cover; cover. Cook 15 minutes, or just until tender.
2 Lift out carefully; drain well, then cut out core. Place cabbage, rounded side up, on a heated serving platter; cut into 6 wedges but leave in shape. Keep warm while cooking steak.
3 Moisten steak with water and sprinkle with meat tenderizer, following label directions. Brush one side with 2 tablespoons of the salad dressing.
4 Broil, following range manufacturer's directions, 3 to 4 minutes; turn; brush other side with remaining salad dressing. Broil 3 to 4 minutes longer for rare, 5 to 6 minutes for medium or until done as you like steak.
5 Remove to cutting board; carve diagonally

1890

into thin slices. Place, overlapping, to cover cabbage completely. Garnish top with 4 more slices rolled up, jelly-roll fashion, and held in place with wooden picks; tuck a sprig of parsley into each roll.

Stuffed Tomato Cups
Miniature "top hats" of cream-puff batter bake atop scooped out tomatoes heaped with cooked peas.
Bake at 400° for 25 minutes. Makes 6 servings

6 medium-size firm tomatoes
1½ cups frozen peas (from a 2-pound bag)
¼ cup water
2 tablespoons butter or margarine
¼ cup sifted all-purpose flour
⅛ teaspoon salt (for batter)
1 egg
1 teaspoon sugar
½ teaspoon salt (for tomatoes)
¼ teaspoon leaf oregano, crumbled

1 Cut off tops of tomatoes; scoop out insides with a teaspoon. Turn cups upside down to drain.
2 Cook peas, following label directions; drain. Keep hot.
3 Heat water and butter or margarine to boiling in a small saucepan. Add flour and the ⅛ teaspoon salt all at once; stir vigorously with a wooden spoon about 2 minutes, or until batter forms a thick smooth ball that follows spoon around pan. Remove from heat at once; cool slightly.
4 Beat in egg until mixture is thick and shiny-smooth.
5 Sprinkle tomato cups with sugar, the ½ teaspoon salt and oregano; fill with hot cooked peas.
6 Spread about 1 tablespoon batter over peas in each tomato, then spoon remaining batter, dividing evenly, in a mound on top. (This gives the "top hat" effect.)
7 Bake in hot oven (400°) 25 minutes, or until topping is puffed and lightly golden and tomato cups are hot.

Gourmet Steak
Makes 6 servings

1 small onion, chopped (¼ cup)
1 small clove of garlic, minced

This is a steak? It is, indeed, Gourmet Steak Platter accompanied by colorful Stuffed Tomato Cups.

½ cup water
2 teaspoons all-purpose flour
1 can (3 or 4 ounces) sliced mushrooms
1 envelope instant beef bouillon
   OR: 1 beef-bouillon cube
1 tablespoon chili sauce
½ teaspoon sugar
1 flank steak (about 2 pounds)
   Unseasoned instant meat tenderizer

1 Heat onion, garlic and water to boiling in small saucepan; cook 10 minutes, or just until liquid evaporates. Lower heat and continue cooking, stirring constantly, 3 to 5 minutes, or until onion browns lightly.
2 Sprinkle flour over and stir in; remove from heat.
3 Drain liquid from mushrooms into 1-cup measure; add water to make 1 cup. (Save

mushrooms for next step.) Stir liquid into onion mixture with instant bouillon or bouillon cube and chili sauce. Cook, stirring constantly, until mixture thickens and boils 1 minute.

4 Stir in mushrooms and sugar. Simmer, uncovered, 10 to 15 minutes to blend flavors.

5 Moisten steak and sprinkle with meat tenderizer, following label directions.

6 Broil, following your range manufacturer's directions, 3 to 4 minutes on each side for rare, 5 to 6 minutes for medium.

7 Remove steak to cutting board; carve diagonally into thin slices. Spoon hot sauce over.

Steak Pizzaiola
Makes 6 servings

1 large onion, chopped (1 cup)
2 cloves of garlic, minced
3 tablespoons olive oil or vegetable oil
1 can (1 pound, 1 ounce) Italian tomatoes
1 teaspoon salt
¼ teaspoon seasoned pepper
  Dash of sugar
1 bone-in chuck steak (about 2 pounds)
  Unseasoned instant meat tenderizer

1 Sauté onion and garlic in oil until soft in large saucepan. Stir in tomatoes, salt, pepper and sugar. Simmer sauce, uncovered, 10 minutes; reserve.

2 While sauce simmers, trim any excess fat from steak and score remaining fat edge every inch. Sprinkle meat with tenderizer, following label directions.

3 Heat a large skillet. Pan-broil steak in skillet, turning once, 5 minutes on each side, or until steak is as done as you like it.

4 Place steak on a cutting board; carve into thin slices. Return to skillet. Stir in reserved tomato sauce; simmer 3 minutes to blend flavors. Serve with hot Italian bread, if you wish.

1892

Garden-Patch Stuffed Steak
Makes 6 servings

1½ pounds boneless round steak (cut about 1 inch thick)
½ cup chopped celery
1 small onion, chopped (¼ cup)
1 tablespoon vegetable oil
1 cup soft bread crumbs (2 slices)
1 egg, beaten

1 package (10 ounces) frozen mixed vegetables, cooked and drained
¼ cup chopped parsley
1 teaspoon salt
⅛ teaspoon pepper
1 envelope instant beef broth
  OR: 1 teaspoon granulated beef bouillon
  Water
2 tablespoons all-purpose flour

1 Trim all visible fat from steak. Cut a pocket crosswise through center of steak to within ¾ inch of edge.

2 Sauté celery and onion in oil until soft in a large skillet. Remove with a slotted spoon. Combine with bread crumbs, egg, drained vegetables, parsley, salt and pepper until well blended in a medium-size bowl.

3 Pack vegetable mixture into steak pocket. Close opening by skewering steak at 1-inch intervals with wooden picks; lace with string and knot at end.

4 Brown steak on both sides in same skillet. Combine 1 cup boiling water and beef broth in a 1-cup measure, stirring until dissolved; add to skillet with steak; lower heat; cover.

5 Simmer, turning steak several times, 1½ hours, or until steak is tender when pierced with a fork.

6 Place meat on a heated serving platter and keep warm. Combine flour and ¼ cup cold water in a 1-cup measure; stir until smooth. Heat liquid in skillet to boiling; stir in flour mixture; continue cooking and stirring until mixture thickens and bubbles 1 minute. Serve gravy over steak.

Sukiyaki
Makes 6 servings

1 chuck steak fillet (about 1½ pounds)
¼ cup vegetable oil
2 medium-size sweet potatoes, pared and thinly sliced
½ pound green beans, tipped and cut in 1-inch pieces
1 small green pepper, halved, seeded and cut into thin strips
1 small sweet red pepper, halved, seeded and cut into thin strips
1 cup thinly sliced celery
½ cup soy sauce
1 cup water
1 small head Chinese cabbage, shredded
1 bunch green onions, trimmed and cut into 2-inch pieces
4 large mushrooms, trimmed and sliced

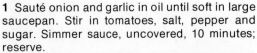

1 Trim all fat from steak; cut meat into very thin strips. (For easier cutting of raw beef, partially freeze steak 1 hour to firm meat.)
2 Heat oil in a large skillet with a cover. Add steak strips and sauté, stirring occasionally, 2 to 3 minutes, or until brown; remove with a slotted spoon and keep warm.
3 Add potatoes, green beans, green and red pepper and celery; sauté 2 to 3 minutes, or until vegetables start to soften.
4 Combine soy sauce and water in a cup; pour over vegetables; cover. Simmer 5 minutes. Stir in shredded cabbage, green onions and mushrooms; cover. Cook 5 minutes longer, or until cabbage wilts and vegetables are crisply tender.
5 Return cooked steak strips to pan and heat until piping-hot. Serve with hot cooked rice and more soy sauce, if you wish.

Chinese Flank Steak
Makes 4 servings

    1 flank steak, weighing about 1½ pounds
    2 tablespoons soy sauce
    1 teaspoon Worcestershire sauce
      Dash of liquid red pepper seasoning
    3 tablespoons vegetable oil
    1 medium-size onion, peeled and sliced
    ½ green pepper, seeded and cut in strips
    1 small clove of garlic, minced
    1 can (3 or 4 ounces) sliced mushrooms
    2 tablespoons cornstarch
    1½ cups beef broth or consommé

1 Slice steak very thin diagonally; place in a bowl. Sprinkle with soy and Worcestershire sauces and red pepper seasoning; toss to mix well.
2 Heat oil until hot in a large frying pan; add seasoned meat. Cook quickly, stirring constantly, until meat loses its pink color; remove from frying pan with a slotted spoon.
3 Stir onion, green pepper and garlic into drippings in pan; sauté until soft. Stir in mushrooms and liquid.
4 Blend cornstarch into beef broth until smooth in a small bowl; stir into vegetables. Cook, stirring constantly, until sauce thickens and boils 3 minutes. Return meat to pan; heat slowly just until hot.

Steak Medallions
Pieces of meat, almost paper-thin, are so tender they can be cut with a fork.
Makes 6 servings

    1½ pounds round beef steak, cut ¾ inch thick
    1 cup unsifted all-purpose flour
    3 tablespoons vegetable oil
    1 large onion, peeled and sliced
    2 teaspoons salt
    ⅛ teaspoon pepper
    ½ cup sliced celery
    2 teaspoons bottled steak sauce
    2 cups water

1 Trim all fat from steak; cut meat into 1½-inch squares. Dip in flour to coat well, then lay on a floured cutting board. Using a wooden mallet or rolling pin, pound each piece, adding more flour as needed, until meat is about ¼ inch thick.
2 Brown, a few pieces at a time, in vegetable oil in a large frying pan; remove. Add onion to pan; sauté until soft; return meat to pan. Add remaining ingredients; cover.
3 Simmer, adding more water, if needed, 1 hour, or until very tender.

Mandarin Beef
Sauté meat quickly, the Oriental way, then combine with soy-seasoned sauce and bake.
Bake at 350° for 1 hour and 10 minutes. Makes 6 to 8 servings

    2 pounds round steak or boneless beef chuck
      Instant unseasoned meat tenderizer
    ¼ cup peanut oil or vegetable oil
    1 large onion, chopped (1 cup)
    2 cups sliced celery
    2 cans (3 or 4 ounces each) sliced mushrooms
    1 can (10½ ounces) condensed cream of chicken soup
    ½ cup water
    ¼ cup soy sauce
    2 cups shredded Chinese cabbage
    ¼ cup toasted slivered almonds (from a 5-ounce can)

1 Moisten meat and sprinkle with tenderizer, following label directions; cut in 2-inch-long strips about ½ inch thick.
2 Brown, a few at a time, in part of the peanut oil or vegetable oil in a large frying pan, adding more oil as needed; spoon into an 8-cup baking dish. Sauté onion just until soft in drippings in frying pan; add with celery to meat.
3 Stir mushrooms and liquid, soup, water and soy sauce into frying pan; heat to boiling; pour over meat mixture; cover.
4 Bake in moderate oven (350°) 1 hour, or until meat is tender; uncover. Place shredded cabbage on top; cover again.
5 Bake 10 minutes longer, or just until cabbage wilts. Just before serving, sprinkle with almonds and serve over rice, if you wish.

STEAKS AND CHOPS

Mushroom Steak Bake

Thick chuck roast makes its own rich gravy as it bubbles in foil.

Bake at 350° for 3 hours, then broil for 5 minutes. Makes 8 servings

1 can or envelope (2 to a package) mushroom-soup mix
1 tablespoon instant minced onion
1 four-pound chuck beef roast, cut 1½ inches thick

1 Combine dry soup mix and onion on a sheet of heavy foil, about 24x18. Roll roast in mixture to coat well, then wrap loosely, sealing edges well. Place on a cookie sheet for easy handling.
2 Bake in moderate oven (350°) 3 hours. Remove from oven; reset temperature control to BROIL.
3 Slit foil across top and fold back, being careful not to let gravy run out. Broil roast 5 minutes, or until top is brown.
4 Carve into ¼-inch-thick slices; serve with gravy from foil package.

Family Steak

Meat bubbles away in a zesty tomato sauce for a savory Old World flavor.

Bake at 350° for 1½ hours. Makes 6 servings

3 pounds chuck steak, cut about 1½ inches thick (often labeled California Roast)
1 envelope (2¼ ounces) spaghetti-sauce mix with tomato
2 cans (about 1 pound each) small whole potatoes, drained
2 cans (about 1 pound each) sliced carrots, drained

1 Brown steak slowly 10 minutes on each side in large heavy frying pan or Dutch oven.
2 While meat browns, prepare spaghetti-sauce mix with water, following label directions; pour over meat; cover.
3 Bake in moderate oven (350°) 1 hour. Place potatoes and carrots in separate piles on top of meat; spoon some of the sauce over each; cover. Bake 30 minutes longer, or until meat is tender.
4 Place meat at one side of heated serving platter; arrange potatoes and carrots around edge. Garnish with parsley, if you wish. Pass sauce in separate bowl to spoon over meat.

Country Casserole Steak

Jumbo steak and sliced smoky sausages bake with vegetables and fruit, then blend with hot macaroni.

Bake at 350° for 2 hours. Makes 4 servings

Family Steak is a Swiss steak, topped with a robust tomato sauce (from a mix) and baked with vegetables.

*Alpine Steak is quick to fix.
It simmers virtually unat-
tended, makes lots of rich
brown gravy to spoon over
fluffy riced potatoes.*

1 boneless chuck beef steak, weighing about
  2 pounds
2 tablespoons all-purpose flour
1 teaspoon salt
¼ teaspoon pepper
1 large onion, peeled, sliced and separated
  into rings
1 cup sliced pared carrots
1 cup sliced celery
1 medium-size tart apple or pear, pared, quartered, cored and sliced
1 package (6 ounces) smoked sausage links,
  sliced ½ inch thick
1 cup water
¼ cup catsup
½ cup chopped parsley
1 cup elbow macaroni (half an 8-ounce package)

1 Trim excess fat from steak. Rub steak with
mixture of flour, salt and pepper. Brown in a
large heavy frying pan over medium heat or in
an electric skillet.
2 Mix onion, carrots, celery and apple or pear

in a greased 12-cup baking dish; top with
browned steak and sausage slices.
3 Stir water, catsup and ¼ cup of the parsley
into drippings in pan; heat to boiling; pour over
meats; cover. (Set remaining ¼ cup parsley
aside for Step 6.)
4 Bake in moderate oven (350°) 2 hours, or until
steak is very tender.
5 While meat mixture bakes, cook macaroni,
following label directions; drain.
6 Remove steak to a cutting board; cut into
½-inch-thick slices. Skim all fat from mixture in
baking dish; stir in macaroni and remaining ¼
cup parsley. Arrange sliced meat on top.

1895

Alpine Steak
Flavorful chuck steak and onion halves with lots
of gravy to spoon over riced potatoes.
Makes 4 servings

4 steaks, cut ½ inch thick, from bone-in or
  boneless chuck roast (about 1½ pounds)
¼ cup unsifted all-purpose flour

STEAKS AND CHOPS

2 teaspoons salt
½ teaspoon pepper
  Few pieces beef suet
4 large yellow onions, halved
2 cups canned mixed vegetable juice
1 teaspoon mixed Italian herbs

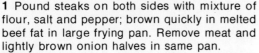

1 Pound steaks on both sides with mixture of flour, salt and pepper; brown quickly in melted beef fat in large frying pan. Remove meat and lightly brown onion halves in same pan.
2 Return steaks to center of pan; arrange onions around edge. Combine mixed vegetable juice and herbs; pour over; cover. Simmer 1 hour, or until meat is tender. Serve with hot riced potatoes.

Family-Best Swiss Steak
Dinner's always a hit with this easy-fix beef choice. And the rich gravy tastes so good over fluffy mashed potatoes!
Makes 4 servings

1 boneless chuck or round beef steak, weighing about 2 pounds
4 tablespoons all-purpose flour
2 tablespoons vegetable oil
1 large onion, chopped (1 cup)
1 cup chopped celery
1 can (8 ounces) tomato sauce
1 cup water
1½ teaspoons salt
1 teaspoon sugar
1 teaspoon leaf marjoram, crumbled
¼ teaspoon pepper

1 Rub steak with flour to coat generously; brown in vegetable oil in a large heavy frying pan or in an electric skillet; remove and set aside for next step.
2 Sauté onion and celery until soft in same frying pan; stir in remaining ingredients. Return steak to pan; cover.
3 Simmer 2 hours, or until meat is very tender. Remove to a heated serving platter; keep hot while fixing gravy.
4 Let gravy stand in pan about a minute, or until fat rises to top; skim off all fat; reheat gravy to boiling.
5 Cut steak into ¼-inch-thick slices; serve with gravy.

Yankee Berry Steak
Meat owes its fresh tart-sweet flavor to a surprise ingredient—cranberry sauce.
Makes 6 servings

1 slice round steak, cut 1 inch thick (about 2 pounds)
3 tablespoons all-purpose flour
1 teaspoon salt
⅛ teaspoon pepper
2 tablespoons vegetable oil
¼ cup water
¼ cup lemon juice
½ teaspoon Worcestershire sauce
1 can (1 pound) whole-fruit cranberry sauce
½ cup chopped celery
1 clove of garlic, minced
1 tablespoon sugar
1 teaspoon grated lemon peel
  Buttered hot rice

1 Rub steak evenly on both sides with mixture of flour, salt and pepper; brown in vegetable oil in a large frying pan.
2 Combine water, lemon juice and Worcestershire sauce in a 1-cup measure; pour over steak; cover. Simmer 1 hour.
3 Mix cranberry sauce, celery, garlic, sugar and lemon peel in a small bowl; spoon on top of steak; cover again. Simmer 1 hour longer, or until steak is tender.
4 Lift steak carefully, without disturbing topping, onto a heated large serving platter; spoon buttered hot rice around edge. Reheat sauce in pan to serve separately, if you wish.

Rolled Stuffed Steakettes
Makes 6 servings

6 slices (½-inch thick each) bottom round
1 large onion, chopped (1 cup)
6 tablespoons vegetable oil
3 cups soft bread crumbs (about 6 slices)
½ cup grated Parmesan cheese
½ cup chopped parsley
1 teaspoon salt
2 tablespoons hot water (for stuffing)
4 tablespoons all-purpose flour
2 envelopes instant beef broth
  OR: 2 teaspoons granulated beef bouillon
1 teaspoon leaf thyme, crumbled
2½ cups water (for gravy)
  Chopped parsley

1 Pound beef slices with a wooden or metal meat mallet, to ¼-inch thickness.

Rolled Stuffed Steakettes are made from medium-priced bottom round but are elegant enough for any party.

2 To make stuffing: Sauté onion in 4 table-spoons of the oil until soft in a large skillet with a cover. Add bread crumbs, Parmesan cheese, parsley, salt and the 2 tablespoons hot water; toss lightly to mix.

3 Spread ¼ cup of the stuffing on each beef slice. Roll up, jelly-roll fashion; secure with wooden picks.

4 Heat remaining 2 tablespoons oil in same skillet. Add beef rolls, turning to brown on all sides; remove to a hot platter; keep warm while making sauce.

5 Stir flour, instant beef broth and thyme into drippings in skillet; cook, stirring constantly, just until bubbly. Stir in the 2½ cups water; continue cooking and stirring, scraping to loosen cooked-on juices in skillet, until gravy thickens and bubbles 1 minute.

6 Return beef rolls to skillet; cover. Simmer 1½ hours, or until tender when pierced with a fork.

7 Place on heated serving platter; spoon a little of the sauce over beef rolls and sprinkle with parsley. Serve remaining sauce separately. If you wish, pipe rosettes of mashed potato around edge of platter, and dot each with a bit of chopped pimiento.

Beef Roulade
Minute steaks with surprising acorn-squash stuffing, gravy made with cranberry juice.
Makes 6 servings

1½ cups stuffing mix (from an 8-ounce package)
  4 tablespoons (½ stick) butter or margarine
1½ cups water
  1 small acorn squash, halved, seeded, pared and shredded
  ¼ cup chopped parsley
  6 individual boneless beefsteaks, each cut ¼ inch thick
  4 tablespoons all-purpose flour
  1 teaspoon salt
  4 tablespoons olive oil or vegetable oil
  1 large onion, chopped (1 cup)
1½ cups cranberry-juice cocktail
  1 envelope instant beef broth
    OR: 1 beef-bouillon cube
  1 teaspoon leaf oregano, crumbled

1 Prepare stuffing mix with butter or margarine and ½ cup of the water, following label directions; stir in squash and parsley.
2 Spread ⅓ cup of the stuffing mixture over each steak; roll up, jelly-roll fashion; hold in place with wooden picks. Mix flour and salt on foil; dust rolls with mixture.
3 Brown rolls in olive oil or vegetable oil in a large frying pan; remove and set aside. Stir onion into drippings in pan; sauté until soft. Stir in cranberry-juice cocktail, remaining 1 cup water, beef broth or bouillon cube and oregano. Cook, stirring constantly and crushing bouillon cube, if used, with a spoon, until mixture thickens and boils 1 minute. Return meat to pan; cover; chill.
4 About 1 hour before serving, heat meat slowly to boiling; cover. Simmer 1 hour, or until meat is tender. Place on a heated serving platter; serve gravy separately to spoon over meat. (If you prefer gravy smooth, place in an electric-blender container; cover; beat until smooth. Return to frying pan and reheat just to boiling.)

1898

Bavarian Steak Rollups
Tucked inside each beef roll is a plump spicy sausage. For pretty serving, arrange atop the sauerkraut in a bowl.
Makes 6 servings

1 slice round steak, cut 1 inch thick (about 2 pounds)
6 sweet Italian sausages
  OR: 6 smoked link sausages (from a 10- or 12-ounce package)
2 tablespoons vegetable oil
1 medium-size onion, chopped (½ cup)
1 can (1 pound, 11 ounces) sauerkraut
1 can (1 pound, 4 ounces) tomatoes
1 tablespoon caraway seeds
1 tablespoon brown sugar
1 teaspoon salt

1 Cut steak into 6 even-size pieces; pound very thin with a wooden mallet or rolling pin. Roll each piece around a sausage, then fasten with one or two wooden picks.
2 Brown slowly in vegetable oil in a large frying pan; remove. Add onion and sauté just until soft.
3 Drain liquid from sauerkraut into frying pan. (Set sauerkraut aside for next step.) Stir in tomatoes, caraway seeds, brown sugar and salt. Return meat to pan; cover.
4 Simmer 1 hour. Spoon sauerkraut in a layer on top of meat; cover again. Simmer 30 minutes longer, or until meat is tender.
5 Spoon sauerkraut into a heated serving dish; arrange meat rolls, spoke fashion, on top. Spoon sauce from pan over. Garnish with a pickled sweet red pepper, if you wish.

Steak Stroganoff
Slices of meat simmer in mushroom sauce, then blend with sour cream for this specialty.
Makes 4 servings

1 slice round steak, cut ½ inch thick (about 1 pound)
  Instant unseasoned meat tenderizer
3 tablespoons all-purpose flour
2 tablespoons vegetable oil
1 large onion, chopped (1 cup)
1 can (6 ounces) sliced mushrooms
2 tablespoons chili sauce
1 teaspoon salt
¼ teaspoon pepper
1 cup dairy (8-ounce carton) sour cream

1 Moisten steak and sprinkle with meat tenderizer, following label directions. Place on cutting board; cut into ¼-inch-thick slices. Shake with flour in a paper bag to coat well.
2 Brown, a few slices at a time, in vegetable

Two original recipes that put reasonable round steak to good use: Yankee Berry Steak, Bavarian Steak Rollups.

oil in a large frying pan; remove. Add onion and sauté just until soft; return meat to pan.

3 Stir in mushrooms and liquid, chili sauce, salt and pepper; cover. Simmer 1 hour, or until meat is tender.

4 Just before serving, stir about 1 cup of the hot meat and sauce mixture into sour cream in a small bowl, then stir back into remaining in frying pan. Heat *very slowly* just until hot. Serve over cooked hot noodles or fluffy rice, if you wish.

VEAL

Veal Chops and Parisian Noodles
Makes 4 servings

3 cups uncooked noodles
1 can (3 or 4 ounces) sliced mushrooms
½ cup milk
2 tablespoons all-purpose flour
2 envelopes instant chicken broth
  OR: 2 chicken-bouillon cubes
1 teaspoon lemon juice
2 tablespoons chopped parsley
4 loin or rib veal chops, cut ¾ inch thick
  Seasoned salt
½ pimiento, cut in thin strips

1 Cook noodles in boiling unsalted water in a kettle, following label directions; drain. Return to kettle.

2 While noodles cook, drain liquid from mushrooms into a 2-cup measure; stir in milk and enough water to make 1¼ cups. (Set mushroom slices aside for kebab garnish for meat.)

3 Stir liquid into flour until smooth in a small saucepan, then stir in chicken broth or bouillon cubes. Cook, stirring constantly and crushing cubes, if using, with a spoon, until sauce thickens and boils 1 minute; stir in lemon juice.

4 Pour mixture over noodles; sprinkle with parsley; toss to mix well; keep hot.

5 Sprinkle chops lightly with seasoned salt; place on rack in broiler pan.

6 Broil, 4 to 6 inches from heat, 8 minutes on each side, or until meat is tender.

7 While meat cooks, thread 4 mushroom slices and a strip of pimiento onto each of 4 kebab sticks. Place chops and noodles on serving plates; stick kebabs into chops.

1900

Veal Chops Supreme
Mushroom sauce seasons the meat as it broils.
Makes 4 servings

1 can (3 or 4 ounces) sliced mushrooms
2 envelopes instant chicken broth
  OR: 2 chicken bouillon cubes
2 tablespoons instant-type flour
1 teaspoon lemon juice
4 loin or rib veal chops, cut ¾ inch thick
1 small sweet red pepper, seeded and cut into 12 rings
2 tablespoons chopped parsley
2 cups hot cooked rice (½ cup uncooked)

1 Drain liquid from mushrooms into a 2-cup measure; add water to make 1¼ cups. Set mushrooms aside.

2 Combine liquid with chicken broth or bouillon cubes and flour in a small saucepan. Cook, stirring constantly and crushing cubes, if using, with a spoon, until sauce thickens and boils 1 minute. Stir in lemon juice.

3 Trim all fat from chops; place chops on rack in broiler pan. Brush with part of the sauce mixture.

4 Broil, 4 to 6 inches from heat, 8 minutes; turn; brush again with more sauce mixture. Broil 6 minutes; place pepper rings on rack beside meat. Continue broiling 2 minutes, or until meat is tender and peppers are heated through.

5 While meat cooks, set aside a few mushroom slices if you wish to garnish the chops, then chop remaining and stir with parsley into remaining sauce; heat until bubbly.

6 When ready to serve, place chops and rice, dividing evenly, on heated serving plates; top rice with pepper rings. (To make garnish, thread saved mushroom slices with sprigs of parsley onto wooden picks; stick into chops.) Serve sauce separately to spoon over meat and rice.

Broiled Veal-Vegetable Platter
Bottled salad dressing seasons mild-flavor veal to broil along with bacon, onion, mushrooms and tomatoes.
Makes 6 servings

1½ to 2 pounds veal cutlet, cut ½-inch thick
¼ cup bottled blue-cheese salad dressing
1 Bermuda onion, peeled and cut in 6 slices
4 tablespoons (½ stick) butter or margarine, melted
  Salt and pepper
3 medium-size tomatoes, halved
6 slices bacon
1 can (3 or 4 ounces) whole mushrooms, drained
1 lemon, cut in 6 wedges

To see just how succulent, tender and flavorful veal can be, give Broiled Veal-Vegetable Platter a try.

1 Place veal on broiler rack; brush top thickly with half of blue-cheese salad dressing. (Set remaining dressing aside for Step 3.)
2 Place onion slices on rack with veal; brush with part of melted butter or margarine; sprinkle lightly with salt and pepper.
3 Broil, 4 to 6 inches from heat, 7 to 8 minutes. Turn veal and onion slices; brush veal with remaining blue-cheese dressing.
4 Place tomato halves, bacon slices and mushrooms alongside veal and onion on rack. (If rack has too open a grid, put mushrooms in a small foil pan.) Brush tomato halves, onion slices and mushrooms with remaining butter or margarine; sprinkle lightly with salt and pepper.
5 Continue to broil, turning bacon once, 7 to 8 minutes longer, or until veal is richly golden, bacon is crisp and tomatoes and mushrooms are heated through.
6 Arrange meats and vegetables on heated serving platter. Carve veal diagonally into ½-inch-thick slices. Serve with lemon wedges to squeeze over veal.

Veal Chops Provençale
Simply brown chops, combine with a savory soup-gravy and let your oven do the rest.
Bake at 350° for 45 minutes. Makes 4 servings

1901

    4 loin or rib veal chops
    1 tablespoon bacon drippings or vegetable oil
    1 small onion, chopped (¼ cup)
    1 can (10½ ounces) condensed cream of
       mushroom soup
    ¼ teaspoon leaf basil, crumbled

1 Brown chops in bacon drippings or vegetable oil in a medium-size frying pan; place in an 8-cup shallow baking dish.
2 Sauté onion just until soft in same pan; stir in soup and basil. Heat, stirring constantly and

scraping cooked-on juices from bottom of pan, just to boiling; pour over chops.

3 Bake in moderate oven (350°) 30 minutes; uncover. Bake 15 minutes longer, or until chops are tender.

Planked Veal Sauté

Variation on a popular platter. Instant mashed potatoes make short work of the border.
Bake potatoes at 400° for 5 minutes. Makes 6 servings

    2 eggs
1½ cups packaged seasoned bread crumbs
1½ pounds veal for scaloppine
    ¼ cup vegetable oil
      Water
    2 packages (10 ounces each) frozen peas and celery
    3 cups prepared instant mashed potatoes
    1 package mushroom gravy mix

1 Separate eggs, placing whites in a pie plate and yolks in a cup for Step 6.

2 Beat whites until frothy; place bread crumbs in a second pie plate. Dip veal pieces into egg whites, then into crumbs to coat well.

3 Brown pieces, a few at a time, in vegetable oil in a large frying pan, adding oil as needed. Remove all meat from pan.

4 Stir 1 cup water into drippings in frying pan; return veal; heat to boiling; cover. Simmer 20 minutes, or until veal is tender.

5 While veal simmers, cook peas and celery, following label directions; keep warm.

6 Beat egg yolks into mashed potatoes; drop by spoonfuls around edge of a large ovenproof platter. (Or press potato mixture through a pastry bag onto platter.)

7 Bake in hot oven (400°) 5 minutes, or until potatoes are tipped with gold.

8 Blend mushroom gravy mix with 1 cup water in a small bowl; stir into hot liquid in frying pan.

Cook, stirring often, 10 minutes, or until gravy thickens. Arrange veal in center of platter with potatoes; spoon vegetables at each end; spoon gravy over veal.

Veal Veneto

Delicate-flavor veal, crisply breaded, hides a filling of melty-cheese.
Makes 4 servings

    4 half-inch-thick slices veal from rump roast (about 1 pound)
    4 slices provolone cheese (from a 6-ounce package)
    1 egg
    ¼ cup milk
    1 cup finely crushed soda crackers (about 20 crackers)
    4 tablespoons (½ stick) butter or margarine

1 Cut veal slices in half; pound paper-thin to make each piece about 4 inches square. Put each 2 together with 1 slice of cheese between, sandwich fashion.

2 Beat egg and milk in a pie plate; put cracker crumbs in second plate. Dip veal sandwiches first into egg mixture, then into crumbs to coat both sides evenly.

3 Sauté slowly in butter or margarine in large frying pan 5 to 7 minutes on each side, or until veal is done and coating is golden-brown.

Easy Veal Parmigiana

Makes 4 to 6 servings

    1 pound veal scaloppine or cubed (waffled) veal cutlets (about 8 pieces)
    2 tablespoons all-purpose flour
    ¼ teaspoon salt

1902

Planked Veal Sauté

Crunchy on the outside, tender on the inside, Quick Veal Cordon Bleu layers ham and cheese with veal.

⅛ teaspoon pepper
2 tablespoons vegetable oil
1 can (about 10 ounces) meatless spaghetti
   sauce
½ cup water
1 beef-bouillon cube
1 package (8 ounces) regular noodles
¼ pound sharp Cheddar cheese, thinly sliced
2 tablespoons grated Parmesan cheese

1 Dip veal pieces into a mixture of flour, salt and pepper to coat both sides; cut into bite-size pieces (kitchen scissors do a quick job); brown in hot oil in large frying pan.
2 Stir in spaghetti sauce, water and bouillon cube; stir to dissolve cube and blend sauce; cover; simmer about 15 minutes, or until veal is tender.
3 While veal simmers, cook noodles, following label directions; drain; place in 6-cup shallow baking dish that will take broiler heat; pour hot veal and sauce over, stirring with fork to coat noodles; top with sliced cheese, then with grated Parmesan cheese.
4 Slide into heated broiler 3 to 5 minutes, or until Cheddar cheese is melted.

●

Quick Veal Cordon Bleu
Scaloppine meat, layered with ham and cheese, bakes fork-tender in just a half hour. Dip mix is the easy seasoner.
Bake at 400° for 30 minutes. Makes 4 servings

2 tablespoons butter or margarine
⅓ cup fine dry bread crumbs
1 packet (2 to an envelope) green-onion dip
   mix
¼ cup cream for whipping
1 pound veal for scaloppine
2 slices cooked ham (from a 5-ounce package), halved
2 slices Muenster cheese (from an 8-ounce
   package), halved

1 Coat bottom and side of a 9-inch pie plate with half of the butter or margarine; sprinkle with half of the bread crumbs. (Set remaining butter or margarine and bread crumbs aside for Step 3.)
2 Mix green-onion dip mix and cream in a second pie plate. Dip half of the veal slices, 1 at a time, in cream mixture to coat one side, then place, coated side down and slightly overlapping, on top of bread crumbs in pie plate. Top with ham and cheese.
3 Dip remaining veal slices in cream mixture; place, coated side up, on top of ham and cheese. Sprinkle with remaining bread crumbs; dot with remaining butter or margarine.
4 Bake in hot oven (400°) 30 minutes, or until veal is tender and golden brown.
5 Serve from its pie-plate baker. Or transfer meat onto a heated serving platter with 2 wide spatulas; garnish with lemon slices sprinkled with paprika and parsley, and serve with hashed browned potatoes, if you wish.

STEAKS AND CHOPS

Breaded Veal Steaks
Use low heat and turn once—these are secrets to a perfect stay-on crumb coating.
Makes 6 servings

      1 egg
      1 teaspoon salt
    ⅛ teaspoon pepper
    ½ cup fine dry bread crumbs
  1½ pounds cube veal steaks or veal tenders
      4 tablespoons vegetable shortening

1 Beat egg with salt and pepper in a pie plate; sprinkle crumbs in second pie plate. Dip veal into egg mixture, then into crumbs to coat both sides well.
2 Sauté *slowly* in shortening in large frying pan 10 to 15 minutes, or until juices appear on top; turn; cook 10 to 15 minutes longer, or until underside is richly browned and meat is tender when pierced with a fork.
3 Arrange on heated platter; serve plain or with a squeeze of fresh lemon juice, if you like.

Veal and Tomatoes Milanese
Strips of melty mozzarella cheese crown tender veal and broiled tomatoes.
Makes 6 servings

      1 egg
      1 teaspoon salt
    ⅛ teaspoon pepper
    ½ cup cracker crumbs
      6 cube veal steaks or veal tenders (about 1½ pounds)
    ¼ cup vegetable shortening
        BROILED GARDEN TOMATOES (recipe follows)
      6 slices bread, crusts removed
        Butter or margarine
      6 slices mozzarella cheese, each cut into 4 strips

1 Beat egg, salt and pepper with a fork in pie plate; sprinkle cracker crumbs into second pie plate. Dip veal into egg mixture, then into crumbs, to coat both sides.
2 Sauté slowly in shortening in large frying pan 5 to 8 minutes on each side, or until richly golden.
3 While veal cooks, fix BROILED GARDEN TO-MATOES. Toast bread; spread with butter or margarine; keep toast hot for Step 5.

4 Place a cooked veal steak on top of each tomato half; arrange 4 strips of cheese over each to form an X; broil just until cheese is melty.
5 Place toast slices in single layer on large serving platter; lift veal-and-tomato stacks onto toast with a broad spatula.

Broiled Garden Tomatoes
They team with veal here—but enjoy them as a separate vegetable, too.
Makes 6 servings

      3 large ripe tomatoes
      2 tablespoons olive oil
  1½ teaspoons sugar
    ½ teaspoon salt
    ⅛ teaspoon pepper

1 Remove stems from tomatoes; cut tomatoes in half crosswise. Arrange, cut side up, on broiler pan; brush with olive oil.
2 Mix sugar, salt and pepper in a cup; sprinkle over tomatoes.
3 Broil about 5 inches from heat, 5 minutes, or just until bubbly on top.

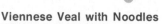

Viennese Veal with Noodles
Makes 6 servings

      6 cube veal steaks or veal tenders (1 to 1½ pounds)
      2 tablespoons vegetable oil
    ½ pound regular noodles
      2 tablespoons butter or margarine
    ¼ cup chopped parsley
      1 can (about 10 ounces) mushroom gravy
    ¼ cup water
      1 cup (8-ounce carton) dairy sour cream

1 Brown veal in vegetable oil in large frying pan 5 minutes on each side.
2 While meat browns, cook noodles, following label directions; drain; stir in butter or margarine and parsley; keep hot.
3 Pour all fat from frying pan; add mushroom gravy and water to veal. Heat to boiling, stirring constantly; simmer 2 to 3 minutes.
4 Stir in sour cream just until blended. Remove pan from heat at once, for sour cream may curdle if allowed to boil.
5 Place veal on heated serving platter; spoon gravy over; surround with hot parsley noodles.

Breaded Veal Steaks, easy to make and easier to eat, are a quickie version of Austria's Wiener Schnitzel. Acorn squash rings, green beans, tiny whole beets and mashed potatoes add the finishing touch.

Veal Continental
Bake at 425° for 25 minutes. Makes 6 servings

  6 veal cube steaks
  4 tablespoons (½ stick) butter or margarine
  1 tablespoon all-purpose flour
  ½ cup milk
  ½ cup water
  1 envelope instant chicken broth
    OR: 1 teaspoon granulated chicken bouillon
  3 tablespoons dry sherry
    Dash of pepper
  2 long slices Swiss cheese, cut in strips
  2 long slices mozzarella cheese, cut in strips

1 Brown veal, part at a time, in butter or margarine in a large frying pan. Place in a single layer in a baking dish, 13x9x2.
2 Stir flour into drippings in pan; stir in milk, water and chicken broth. Cook, stirring constantly, until mixture thickens and boils 1 minute. Stir in sherry and pepper; heat to boiling; pour over veal. Arrange Swiss- and mozzarella-cheese strips over all.
3 Bake in hot oven (425°) 25 minutes, or until cheeses melt and brown slightly.

LAMB

Gourmet Lamb Chops
Makes 6 servings

  6 loin lamb chops, cut about 1 inch thick
  3 lamb kidneys
    Salt and pepper
  6 large fresh mushrooms
  6 pickled sweet red peppers

1 Trim all fat from chops. Split each kidney; snip out tubes and white membrane with scissors.
2 Place chops on broiler rack; broil, following range manufacturer's directions, 8 to 10 minutes for medium; turn. Place kidneys on rack with chops; broil both, turning kidneys once, 8 to 10 minutes. Sprinkle all lightly with salt and pepper.
3 While meat broils, wash mushrooms; cut off stems to within ¼ inch of cap; flute this way: With sharp thin-blade knife, mark center of each cap. Starting here, make a curved cut about ⅛ inch deep to edge. Repeat around cap to make 12 evenly spaced cuts. Now make a sec-

1905

STEAKS AND CHOPS

Gourmet Lamb Chops are topped with lamb kidney kebabs.

ond curved cut just behind each line, slanting knife in so you can lift out a narrow strip. Heat caps in hot water in small frying pan, 2 to 3 minutes, or just until the cuts open up slightly.
4 Thread 1 pickled pepper, half a broiled kidney and 1 mushroom cap, kebab style, on each long wooden pick. Stick into each chop on heated serving plate.

Company Grill
Makes 6 servings

6 *loin lamb chops,* cut ¾ to 1 inch thick (about 2 pounds)*
SAVORY BASTING SAUCE *(recipe follows)*
6 *chicken livers*
6 *small stuffed green olives*
3 *large ripe peaches, unpeeled*
2 *tablespoons butter or margarine*

1 Cut fat edges of lamb chops in several places to keep chops from curling; brush with SAVORY BASTING SAUCE; place on grill over hot coals; grill, basting with sauce, 5 to 8 minutes; turn and grill, basting often, 5 to 8 minutes longer, or until done as you like lamb.
2 Cut each chicken liver into 4 or 5 pieces; divide and thread onto 6 small skewers; end each with an olive; brush all with sauce; place on grill around edge (if wire grids are wide apart, set skewers on a sheet of foil pierced with small holes for sauce to run through); grill, turning and basting often with sauce. (Delicate chicken livers cook quickly—don't overcook.)
3 Cut peaches in half; remove pits; fill each hollow with 1 teaspoon butter or margarine; place on edge of grill to heat and melt butter.
4 Top each lamb chop with a peach half, cut side up; lay a chicken-liver kebab across each peach.

* Or buy thriftily priced meaty shoulder lamb chops.

SAVORY BASTING SAUCE—Combine ½ cup vegetable oil, 2 tablespoons lemon juice, 1 teaspoon Worcestershire sauce, 1 crushed clove of garlic and ¼ teaspoon crushed leaf rosemary in small saucepan; heat to boiling to blend flavors; keep hot for basting meat on grill. Makes ⅔ cup.

1906

Mint-Glazed Lamb Chops
Makes 4 servings

Sprinkle 8 rib lamb chops with salt and pepper; broil 4 inches from heat about 6 minutes on each side, or until done as you like lamb. Brush tops lightly with mint jelly.

Currant-Glazed Lamb Chops
Makes 6 servings

Pan-broil 6 shoulder lamb chops slowly in large frying pan 20 to 25 minutes, or until tender. Pour off all fat. While chops cook, combine ¼ cup currant jelly, ¼ cup water, 1 tablespoon lemon juice and 2 tablespoons chopped fresh mint in a cup; pour over chops. Simmer, uncovered, 5 to 8 minutes, or just until liquid evaporates and chops are glazed.

Lamb Chops Pakistani
Makes 4 servings

4 shoulder lamb chops (from combination package)
1 tablespoon butter or margarine
1 medium-size onion, chopped
1 cup uncooked regular rice
½ cup green grapes, seeded
¼ cup chopped dried apricots
¼ cup roasted peanuts
1 teaspoon salt
½ teaspoon ground ginger
¼ teaspoon ground cloves
¼ teaspoon pepper
Crushed seeds from 2 cardamoms
1 cup orange juice
1 cup water

1 Trim fat from chops; melt butter or margarine in large heavy frying pan with tight-fitting cover; brown chops on both sides; remove.
2 Sauté onion until tender in remaining fat in pan; stir in rice, grapes, apricots, peanuts, salt, ginger, cloves, pepper, crushed cardamom seeds, orange juice and water; arrange chops on top; cover.

3 Heat to boiling; reduce heat; simmer 40 minutes, or until chops and rice are tender and liquid is absorbed.

Broiled Curried Lamb Steaks
Makes 4 servings

2 lamb steaks, about 1 inch thick (cut from half a leg of lamb)
¾ cup canned pineapple juice
½ teaspoon ground ginger
½ teaspoon curry powder
Seeds from 1 cardamom pod, crushed*

1 Place steaks in single layer in shallow dish; mix pineapple juice, ginger, curry powder and crushed cardamom and pour over steaks; cover; chill, turning once, at least 12 hours.
2 Drain; broil steaks, 4 inches from heat, 6 minutes on each side for medium-done; cut each in half.

* Remove the little black seeds from cardamom pod; place between sheets of wax paper or foil and roll with rolling pin.

1907

Skillet Lamb and Rice

Low-priced lamb cooks with fruit-seasoned rice for this gourmetlike dish.
Makes 4 servings

4 shoulder lamb chops (from combination package)
1 medium-size onion, chopped (½ cup)
1 cup uncooked regular rice
¼ cup raisins
2 tablespoons chopped parsley
1 teaspoon salt
1 cup orange juice
1 cup water

1 Trim fat from chops; brown chops quickly in heavy frying pan; remove. Drain all but 1 tablespoon fat from pan.
2 Stir in onion, and sauté until soft; stir in rice; sauté until soft; stir in rice; sauté just until golden; mix in remaining ingredients.
3 Arrange browned chops on top; cover. Simmer 40 minutes, or until chops and rice are tender and liquid is absorbed.

PORK AND HAM

Onion-Pork Sauté

Browned chops simmer sweetly tender; creamy gravy is the easiest ever.
Makes 6 servings

6 rib pork chops, cut ½ inch thick
1 large onion, peeled and cut in 6 slices
1 envelope instant beef broth
  OR: 1 beef-flavor bouillon cube
¼ cup hot water
½ cup evaporated milk

1 Brown chops in a large frying pan or an electric skillet; top each with a slice of onion. Dissolve beef broth or bouillon cube in hot water in a 1-cup measure; pour over chops; cover.
2 Simmer 40 minutes, or until chops are tender. Remove with onions and keep hot. Sprinkle onions with paprika, if you wish.
3 Stir evaporated milk into drippings in pan. Heat, stirring constantly, until bubbly hot. Serve in separate bowl to spoon over chops.

Bermuda Pork Chops

Makes 4 servings

4 loin or rib pork chops, cut ¾ inch thick
¼ teaspoon ground allspice
¼ cup firmly packed brown sugar
1½ teaspoons salt
1 Bermuda onion, peeled, sliced and separated into rings
1 tablespoon chopped parsley
  GOLDEN HOMINY (recipe follows)

1 Trim all but a thin layer of fat from chops. Sprinkle both sides of chops with allspice and rub into meat.
2 Brown chops in a small amount of hot fat from trimmings in medium-size heavy frying pan; drain all fat from pan.
3 Mix brown sugar and salt in a cup; sprinkle half over chops. Top with onion rings; sprinkle remaining sugar mixture over.
4 Cover lightly; cook over low heat 45 minutes, or until chops are tender.
5 Remove chops, with onion rings on top, to a heated serving platter; sprinkle with parsley; serve with GOLDEN HOMINY.
  GOLDEN HOMINY—Drain 1 can (1 pound, 13 ounces) hominy; stir into drippings in frying pan. Heat, stirring often, 3 to 5 minutes, or until piping-hot. Season with salt and pepper. Makes 4 servings.

Creole Pork Chops

Makes 6 servings

6 rib or shoulder pork chops, cut about ¾ inch thick
1 cup uncooked regular rice
1 medium-size onion, chopped
½ cup diced celery
2 cans (about 1 pound each) tomatoes
1 teaspoon salt
½ teaspoon leaf thyme, crumbled
¼ teaspoon pepper

1 Trim excess fat from chops; melt trimmings to make 2 tablespoons fat in large heavy frying pan; discard trimmings; toast rice in fat, stirring often; remove rice from pan.
2 Brown chops in same pan; remove; cook onion and celery in remaining fat until golden.
3 Return chops to pan; spoon rice between; add tomatoes and seasonings; cover.
4 Cook over low heat about 50 minutes, or until chops are tender.

Oriental Pork and Peppers

Makes 6 servings

8 thin pork chops, weighing about 1½ pounds
1 small onion, chopped (¼ cup)
1 clove of garlic, minced
3 tablespoons vegetable oil

1908

Because pork chops must always be cooked well done, they are best when braised. Shown: Curried Pork Chops.

1 envelope instant chicken broth
  OR: 1 teaspoon granulated chicken bouillon
1 cup water
1 can (1 pound) bean sprouts, drained and rinsed
2 medium-size green peppers, halved, seeded and chopped
2 medium-size tomatoes, chopped
1 teaspoon salt
3 tablespoons cornstarch
3 tablespoons soy sauce
4 cups cooked rice

1 Trim fat and bone from pork chops; cut meat into julienne strips.
2 Sauté onion and garlic in vegetable oil until soft in a large frying pan. Stir in pork; sauté, stirring once, 5 minutes, or until brown.
3 Stir in chicken broth, ¾ cup of the water, bean sprouts, green peppers, tomatoes and salt. Heat to boiling, then cook 3 minutes, or until peppers are crisply tender.
4 Mix cornstarch with remaining ¼ cup water and soy sauce until smooth in a cup; stir into mixture in frying pan. Cook, stirring constantly, until mixture thickens and boils 3 minutes. Serve over rice.

Curried Pork Chops
Makes 4 servings

8 thin pork chops
  Dash of salt
  Dash of pepper
1 teaspoon vegetable shortening
1 large onion, chopped (1 cup)
1 tablespoon curry powder
1 cup catsup
½ cup Worcestershire sauce
1 tablespoon cider vinegar
¾ cup water

1 Sprinkle pork chops with salt and pepper; brown in shortening in a large frying pan; remove and set aside.
2 Stir onion and curry powder into drippings in pan; sauté until onion is soft. Stir in catsup, Worcestershire sauce and vinegar; return chops to pan. Heat slowly to boiling; simmer 15 minutes.
3 Stir in water; cover. Simmer 30 minutes, or until meat is very tender.

1909

STEAKS AND CHOPS

Skillet Pork Orientale
Makes 6 servings

    6 pork chops, cut ½ inch thick
    1 teaspoon curry powder
    1 envelope instant chicken broth
    1 can (1 pound) small whole potatoes,
      drained
    1 can (about 1 pound) small boiled onions,
      drained
 1½ cups water
    1 can (about 1 pound) sliced carrots, drained
    ½ head Chinese cabbage, washed and cut
      crosswise into 6 slices
    ½ teaspoon salt
    ⅛ teaspoon pepper
    2 tablespoons chopped parsley

1 Trim fat and bone from each chop. Cut meat into thin slices.
2 Melt a few of the fat trimmings in a large frying pan; stir in curry powder and chicken broth. Add meat and brown; push to one side.
3 Add potatoes and onions; sauté 5 minutes. Stir in 1 cup water; cover. Simmer 30 minutes, or until pork is almost tender.
4 Place carrots and Chinese cabbage on top; sprinkle with salt, pepper and parsley. Pour in remaining ½ cup water; cover. Cook 15 minutes longer, or until pork is tender and cabbage is crisply tender.
5 Spoon meat and vegetables into a serving bowl; pass pan juices in a separate bowl to spoon over, if you wish.

Spanish Skillet Pork
Makes 6 servings

    6 fully cooked smoked pork chops
    1 tablespoon vegetable oil
    2 cans (1 pound each) Spanish rice
    1 medium-size green pepper, halved, seeded
      and cut into ¼-inch-wide strips

1 Brown chops in vegetable oil in a large frying pan 5 minutes on each side; remove from pan; pour off any drippings.
2 Spoon Spanish rice into pan; arrange chops, then green-pepper strips on top; cover. Simmer 10 minutes, or until bubbly-hot and peppers are tender. Serve from skillet.

Pork Cutlets Bordeaux
Makes 4 servings

    4 pork cutlets, cut ¼ inch thick and weighing
      about 1¼ pounds
    1 egg

    1 cup fine dry bread crumbs
    2 tablespoons butter or margarine
    2 tablespoons vegetable oil
    1 cup dry red wine
    2 envelopes instant chicken broth
      OR: 2 teaspoons granulated chicken bouillon
    ½ teaspoon salt
    ⅛ teaspoon pepper

1 Trim all fat from pork cutlets.
2 Beat egg slightly in a pie plate; place bread crumbs on wax paper. Dip cutlets into beaten egg, then into crumbs to coat well; let stand about 20 minutes uuntil coating sets.
3 Brown cutlets slowly, turning once, in butter or margarine and vegetable oil in a large frying pan; remove from pan.
4 Stir wine, chicken broth, salt and pepper into pan; heat, scraping brown bits from bottom of pan, to boiling; simmer 1 minute.
5 Place cutlets in sauce; cover. Simmer 45 minutes, or until cutlets are tender. Place on a heated large serving platter; spoon sauce from pan over top.

Curry-Glazed Pork Chops
Each tender thick chop sparkles with a spicy fruit-rich sauce.
Bake at 400° for 40 minutes. Makes 8 servings

    8 rib or loin pork chops, cut ½ inch thick
    1 large onion, chopped (1 cup)
    2 tablespoons all-purpose flour
    2 tablespoons brown sugar
    1 tablespoon curry powder
    1 teaspoon salt
    1 teaspoon ground cinnamon
    1 beef-flavor bouillon cube
      OR: 1 envelope instant beef bouillon
    1 cup water
    2 tablespoons catsup
    1 jar (about 4 ounces) baby-pack strained
      apples-and-apricots
    ¼ cup flaked coconut

1 Trim any excess fat from chops. Brown chops in a large frying pan, then place in a single layer in a baking pan.
2 Sauté onion in drippings until soft in same pan. Blend in flour, brown sugar, curry powder, salt and cinnamon; cook, stirring constantly, until bubbly; stir in remaining ingredients.

1910

Curry-Glazed Pork chops are a marvelous sweet-sour recipe sauced with baby-pack apples-and-apricots. ▶

Couldn't be simpler or more sensational! Onion-Glazed Pork Chops seasoned with can of dry onion-soup mix.

1912

3 Heat, stirring constantly, to boiling, crushing bouillon cube, if using, with a spoon, then simmer, uncovered, 5 minutes, or until thick. Spoon half over chops.
4 Bake in hot oven (400°) 20 minutes; spoon on remaining sauce. Bake 20 minutes longer, or until tender and richly glazed.

●

Mustard-Glazed Pork Chops
Bake at 350° for 45 minutes. Makes 6 servings

   6 *lean pork chops, cut 1 inch thick*
   1 *large onion, peeled and cut into 6 slices*
  ½ *teaspoon salt*
    Dash of pepper
   1 *envelope instant chicken broth*
    OR: 1 chicken-bouillon cube
   2 *teaspoons prepared mustard*
  ¼ *cup water*

1 Trim off all fat from chops; brown chops in a large frying pan.
2 Place onion slices in a single layer in a large shallow baking pan; top each with a browned chop; sprinkle with salt and pepper.
3 Combine chicken broth or bouillon cube, mustard and water in a cup. (If using cube,

crush with a spoon.) Drizzle mixture over chops; cover.
4 Bake in moderate oven (350°) 45 minutes, or until chops are tender.
5 Place each on its onion slice on a heated serving plate. Garnish with a vegetable kebab, radish rose and a spear of Belgian endive.
Note: To make vegetable kebabs, thread 4 thin rounds of green pepper, 2 slices of water chestnut and 4 tiny pickled onions each onto wooden picks or skewers.

●

Onion-Glazed Pork Chops
Soup mix both seasons and glazes the meat.
Bake at 350° for 1½ hours. Makes 6 servings

   1 *can (2 to a package) dry onion-soup mix*
   2 *cups water*
   6 *pork chops, cut ¾ inch thick*

1 Combine onion-soup mix and water in small saucepan; heat to boiling; simmer 5 minutes.
2 Place pork chops in single layer in baking dish, 13x9x2; spoon onion soup over.
3 Bake, uncovered, in moderate oven (350°) 1½ hours, or until chops are tender and richly glazed.

4 Arrange chops on heated serving platter. Pour soup drippings from pan into a small saucepan; skim off fat; heat to boiling. Serve in bowl to spoon over chops.

Pork Chops Cacciatore
Spaghetti-sauce mix in an envelope gives a zesty flavor to baked pork chops.
Bake at 350° for 1 hour and 15 minutes. Makes 6 servings

6 *loin, rib or shoulder pork chops*
1 *Bermuda onion, cut in 6 slices*
2 *tablespoons brown sugar*
1 *envelope spaghetti-sauce mix*
2 *cans (about 1 pound each) tomatoes*

1 Brown pork chops in large frying pan; arrange in single layer in shallow 8-cup baking dish. Top each chop with an onion slice; sprinkle with brown sugar.
2 Blend spaghetti-sauce mix into drippings in frying pan; stir in tomatoes; heat to boiling, stirring constantly. Spoon around chops and onions; cover.
3 Bake in moderate oven (350°) 1 hour; uncover; bake 15 minutes longer, or until chops are tender.

Harvest Moon Pork Towers
Buy thin chops—sometimes labeled ''Breakfast,'' ''Brown-and-serve,'' or ''Pan-fry''—to stack three high with potato stuffing.
Bake at 350° for 1 hour. Makes 6 servings

2 *medium-size potatoes, pared and cut up*
2 *tablespoons butter or margarine*
2 *cups small bread cubes (4 slices)*
1½ *teaspoons poultry seasoning*
1 *teaspoon salt*
⅛ *teaspoon pepper*
18 *thin pork chops*
½ *teaspoon paprika*

1 Cook potatoes, covered, in boiling salted water in a medium-size saucepan 20 minutes, or until tender; lift out with a slotted spoon and place in a large bowl.
2 Stir in butter or margarine, bread cubes, poultry seasoning, salt, pepper and 2 tablespoons potato water.
3 Brown pork chops, a few at a time, in a large frying pan; remove.
4 Stack each three chops with potato stuffing between, using 2 generous tablespoonfuls stuffing for each layer; place in a large shallow baking dish; cover.
5 Bake in moderate oven (350°) 50 minutes;

uncover. Baste chops with drippings in dish; sprinkle with paprika.
6 Bake 10 minutes longer, or until chops are tender and lightly browned.

Autumn Pork Stacks
Grated carrots, whole-kernel corn and thick slices of onion are layered between chops, then baked.
Bake at 350° for 1½ hours. Makes 6 servings

12 *loin or rib pork chops, cut ¾ inch thick*
3 *large carrots, pared and grated*
1 *large Bermuda onion, peeled and cut in 6 thick slices*
1 *can (12 ounces) Mexican-style corn*
½ *cup water*
2 *teaspoons salt*
1 *teaspoon leaf marjoram, crumbled*
½ *teaspoon sugar*
¼ *teaspoon ground cardamom*

1 Trim any excess fat from chops. Brown chops, part at a time, in a large frying pan; place 6 in a large shallow baking dish to make a layer.
2 Layer carrots, a slice of onion and corn over each; top with remaining 6 chops.
3 Stir water, salt, marjoram, sugar and cardamom into drippings in frying pan; heat to boiling, scraping browned bits from bottom of pan; pour over chops; cover.
4 Bake in moderate oven (350°) 1½ hours, or until chops and vegetables are tender. Lift each stack onto a heated serving platter; spoon juices from dish over chops.

Barbecued Pork Chops and Kraut
Bake at 350° for 1 hour. Makes 4 servings

4 *loin pork chops, each cut ¾ inch thick (about 1½ pounds)*
1 *can (1 pound, 11 ounces) sauerkraut, drained*
1 *medium-size apple, halved, cored and diced*
2 *tablespoons catsup*
2 *tablespoons water*
1 *tablespoon dark corn syrup*
1 *teaspoon salt*
¼ *teaspoon pepper*

1 Trim fat from chops. Brown slowly on both sides in a frying pan.
2 Combine sauerkraut and apple in a shallow

1913

Duxbury Chops and Dressing—half a dozen thick pork loin chops on a bed of cranberry-orange stuffing.

8-cup baking dish; toss to mix. Arrange browned chops on top.

3 Stir catsup, water, corn syrup, salt and pepper into frying pan; heat slowly, stirring constantly, to boiling. Pour over chops; cover baking dish tightly.

4 Bake in moderate oven (350°) 30 minutes; uncover. Bake 30 minutes longer, or until chops are tender.

Pork Steaks Diable

Meat bakes in a peppy sauce; olives make an exotic seasoner.

Bake at 350° for 1 hour. Makes 6 servings

6 pork shoulder steaks, cut ½ inch thick (2½ to 3 pounds)
1 clove of garlic, peeled
1 tablespoon prepared mustard

2 large onions, each cut into 3 thick slices
1 jar (3 ounces) stuffed green olives
1 tablespoon brown sugar
1 tablespoon cider vinegar
¼ teaspoon pumpkin-pie spice

1 Brown steaks slowly in their own fat with whole clove of garlic in a large frying pan; place in a single layer in a shallow baking pan. Discard garlic; pour off fat from pan.
2 Spread mustard over steaks; top with onion slices.
3 Drain liquid from olives into a 2-cup measure; chop olives. Add water to liquid to make 1 cup; stir in brown sugar, vinegar and pumpkin-pie spice.
4 Heat to boiling in the same frying pan, scraping any browned bits from bottom. Pour over onion slices and pork; sprinkle with chopped olives; cover.
5 Bake in moderate oven (350°) 45 minutes; uncover. Bake 15 minutes longer, or until pork is tender.

Duxbury Chops and Dressing
Bake at 350° for 1½ hours. Makes 6 servings

6 cups cubed white bread
6 loin pork chops, cut 1 inch thick
1 large onion, chopped (1 cup)
1 cup thinly sliced celery
6 tablespoons (¾ stick) butter or margarine
1 envelope instant chicken broth
   OR: 1 teaspoon granulated chicken bouillon
1 cup water
½ cup cranberry-orange relish (from a 14-ounce jar)
1 can (6 ounces) chopped mushrooms, drained
½ teaspoon salt
½ teaspoon leaf thyme, crumbled
½ teaspoon leaf sage, crumbled
¼ teaspoon pepper

1 Place bread cubes in a shallow pan; toast in moderate oven (350°) 20 minutes, or until golden.
2 Trim all fat from pork chops. Sauté a few of the trimmings in a large frying pan; remove and discard. Place chops in drippings in pan; sauté slowly, turning once, until richly browned; remove from pan and keep warm.
3 Sauté onion and celery in butter or margarine until soft in same pan; stir in chicken broth, water, cranberry-orange relish, mushrooms, salt, thyme, sage and pepper; heat to boiling. Pour over bread cubes; toss until evenly moist. Spoon into a lightly greased baking pan,

13x9x2. Arrange browned chops in a single layer on top; cover.
4 Bake in moderate oven (350°) 1 hour and 30 minutes, or until chops are tender.
5 Remove chops from pan; spoon dressing onto a heated large serving platter; stand chops around edge. Garnish with celery leaves, if you wish.

Pocketbook Pork Chops
Each holds a fresh mushroom stuffing lightly seasoned with salad herbs.
Bake at 350° for 1½ hours. Makes 6 servings

6 loin pork chops, cut 1 inch thick
1 pound fresh mushrooms, washed, trimmed and chopped (6 cups)
1 cup sliced celery
4 tablespoons (½ stick) butter or margarine
2 tablespoons chopped parsley
1 teaspoon mixed salad herbs
1 teaspoon salt
1 egg, beaten
2 cups coarse unsalted cracker crumbs
   Seasoned pepper

1 Trim excess fat from chops; then make a slit in each to form a pocket.
2 Sauté mushrooms and celery in butter or margarine in a large frying pan 5 minutes; stir in parsley, salad herbs and salt; cool slightly. Stir in beaten egg and cracker crumbs.
3 Spoon about ⅓ cup into pocket in each chop, packing it in lightly. (Stuffing is moist enough to stay in place without skewering chops.) Place chops in a single layer in a large shallow baking dish; sprinkle lightly with seasoned pepper. Spoon remaining stuffing into a greased small baking dish; cover.
4 Bake chops in moderate oven (350°) 1½ hours, or until tender. Bake stuffing in same oven 1 hour, or until heated through.

Dixie Pork Chop Roast
For this handsome dinner showpiece, take advantage of a special on loin of pork, then cut it into chops for stuffing.
Roast at 325° for 3 hours. Makes 6 servings

1 loin of pork, weighing about 5 pounds
½ cup uncooked regular rice
½ cup chopped dried apricots
1 envelope instant beef broth
¼ cup coarsely chopped pecans
¼ teaspoon ground mace
   GOLDEN APRICOT GLAZE (recipe follows)

1915

1 Ask your meatman to cut pork loin into chops, keeping them in order.

2 Combine rice, apricots and instant beef broth in a medium-size saucepan; add water and cook, following label directions for rice; remove from heat. Stir in pecans and mace with a fork.

3 Insert a long skewer through each end of chops to hold them together; place on a rack in a roasting pan. Spoon rice stuffing between chops, dividing evenly. If using a meat thermometer, insert into meaty center of one chop without touching bone or stuffing; cover tops of chops loosely with foil.

4 Roast in slow oven (325°) 2½ hours, or until thermometer registers 170°; uncover.

5 Brush with GOLDEN APRICOT GLAZE to coat chops thickly. Continue roasting, basting several times with remaining apricot mixture, ½ hour longer, or until thermometer registers 185° and meat is richly glazed.

6 Remove to a heated large serving platter; pull out skewers. Garnish platter with canned apricot halves and curly endive, if you wish.

GOLDEN APRICOT GLAZE—Combine ¾ cup apricot preserves, 4 teaspoons lemon juice and ¼ teaspoon ground cloves in a small saucepan; heat, stirring constantly, just to boiling.

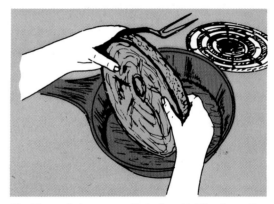

Heat heavy frying pan until sizzling. Holding ham slice in your hands, rock back and forth on slashed fat as pictured, until edge is brown.

desired, brown outside edge of fat as shown. Place slice on rack in heated broiler with top about 4 inches from heat.

Broil UNCOOKED (cook-before-eating) slice 10 minutes on each side.

Broil COOKED (ready-to-eat) slice 5 minutes on each side. If desired, decorate.

HOW TO COOK HAM STEAK

Baked Ham Steak
Slash fat on a 1-inch slice of uncooked (cook-before-eating) or cooked (ready-to-eat) ham. If desired, brown outside edge of fat as shown. Place ham slice in shallow baking pan.

Bake UNCOOKED (cook-before-eating) slice in slow oven (325°) for 25 to 30 minutes per pound.

Heat COOKED (ready-to-eat) slice in moderate oven (350°) 15 to 20 minutes, or just until hot.

To brown top, slide cook-before-eating or ready-to-eat ham slice in broiler about 4 inches from heat for 5 minutes. If desired, decorate.

Broiled Ham Steak
Slash fat on a 1-inch slice of uncooked (cook-before-eating) or cooked (ready-to-eat) ham. If

HOW TO DECORATE A HAM STEAK

The decorations are put on after the steak has been cooked—just before serving. Here's how:

CHEESE-APRICOT—Drain syrup from 1 can whole apricots; remove pits from fruit. Blend ½ cup (half an 8-ounce container) cottage cheese with 2 teaspoons prepared horseradish and salt to taste. Fill drained apricots with seasoned cheese mixture. Arrange 3 on top of cooked ham slice with a few sprigs of watercress; serve remaining stuffed apricots in separate dish.

CHERRY-ALMOND—This decoration is made with halves of maraschino or candied cherries and quartered almonds. (Almonds cut easiest if allowed to stand a few minutes in hot water.) Arrange fruit and nuts to make flower designs.

ORANGE-CLOVE—Cut skin and white membrane from orange; slice; stud each slice with a few whole cloves. Overlap in line down middle of cooked ham slice.

MUSHROOM-PARSLEY—Slice medium-size mushrooms through crown and stem to make umbrella-shape pieces. Use about 5 mushrooms in all. Sauté in butter or margarine in frying pan just until golden, turning once. Arrange in over-

1917

Dixie Pork Chop Roast, a five-pound-line-up of loin chops stuffed with rice, apricots, chopped pecans.

lapping ring on cooked ham slice; fill center of ring with perky parsley.

●

Fruited Ham Steak
Bake at 350° for 45 minutes. Makes 4 servings

1 *slice cook-before-eating or fully cooked ham, cut 1 inch thick*
½ *cup firmly packed light brown sugar*
½ *teaspoon dry mustard*
1 *can (about 9 ounces) sliced pineapple*
1 *can (8 ounces) greengage plums*

1 Trim fat edge of ham, then score; place in a baking pan; top with mixture of brown sugar and mustard.
2 Drain syrup from pineapple; measure and add enough syrup from plums to make 1 cup; pour around ham.
3 Bake in moderate oven (350°) 30 minutes.
4 Halve pineapple slices; place along with plums on top of ham; spoon syrup from pan over. Bake, basting 2 or 3 times, 15 minutes longer, or until fruits are heated through and glazed.

●

Kansas Ham Steak
For a bright change, double corn stuffing bakes on top of a thick steak.
Bake at 350° for 40 minutes. Makes 4 servings

1 *fully cooked ham steak, cut 1 inch thick (about one pound)*
1 *small onion, chopped (¼ cup)*
2 *tablespoons butter or margarine*
3 *flat cornmeal cakes*
1 *can (12 ounces) Mexican-style corn, drained*
1 *egg, slightly beaten*
1 *teaspoon dry mustard*
  Dash of pepper
2 *envelopes mushroom gravy mix*
  Water
¼ *cup dry sherry*

1 Trim any excess fat from ham; score fat edge; place in a shallow baking pan.
2 Sauté onion in butter or margarine until soft in a large frying pan; remove from heat. Crumble corn cakes into frying pan; add corn, egg, mustard and pepper; toss lightly to mix. Spoon on top of ham; cover pan tightly with foil.
3 Bake in moderate oven (350°) 40 minutes.
4 While ham bakes, prepare mushroom gravy mix with water, following label directions; stir in sherry.
5 Lift ham with stuffing onto a heated large serving platter; carve into ½-inch-thick slices, cutting through stuffing. Serve gravy separately to spoon over all.

●

Ham Steak Kingston
A spicy sauce flavored with gingersnaps accents smoky ham and tangy pineapple.
Bake at 325° for 1½ hours. Makes 4 servings

1 *slice ready-to-eat ham, cut about 1 inch thick*
1 *can (1 pound, 4 ounces) pineapple spears*
¼ *cup firmly packed brown sugar*
1 *teaspoon dry mustard*
¼ *teaspoon ground allspice*
2 *gingersnaps*

1 Place ham steak in shallow baking dish or pie plate.
2 Drain syrup from pineapple spears into 2-cup measure. (There will be about 1 cup.) Stir in brown sugar, mustard and allspice; pour over ham.
3 Bake in slow oven (325°) 1 hour; lay pineapple spears over ham; baste with syrup in dish; bake 30 minutes longer, or until top is glazed.
4 Remove ham and pineapple to heated serving platter; pour liquid into small saucepan; let stand about a minute, or until fat rises to top; skim. Crumble in gingersnaps; heat, stirring constantly, until sauce thickens slightly. Serve with ham.

1918

INDEX TO RECIPES IN THIS VOLUME

1919

Kansas Ham Steak 1918
Mustard-Glazed Pork Chops 1912
Onion-Glazed Pork Chops 1912
Onion-Pork Sauté 1908
Oriental Pork and Peppers 1908
Pocketbook Pork Chops 1915
Pork Chops Cacciatore 1913
Pork Cutlets Bordeaux 1910
Pork Sauté
Pork Steaks Diable 1914
Skillet Pork Orientale 1910
Spanish Skillet Pork 1910

Eggs and Cheese:
Eggs Mimosa 1862

Vegetables:
Broiled Garden Tomatoes 1904
Buttered Onion Rings 1877
Mushrooms Royale 1886
Skillet Pepper Rings 1884
Stuffed Tomato Cups 1890

Rice and Pasta:
Golden Hominy 1908
Homemade Egg Noodles 1840

Breads:
Herb Bread Chunks 1868
Marrow Balls 1862

Sauces and Gravies:
Chives Butter 1882
Cream Steak Gravy 1888
Golden Apricot Glaze 1917
Sauce Continental 1877
Savory Basting Sauce 1906
Zippy Tomato Sauce 1877

Desserts:
Apple-Cinnamon Ice Cream 1807
Banana Splits Royale 1815
Berry Fudge Sundaes 1811
Biscuit Tortoni 1807
Brandied Peach Ice Cream 1806
Brazilian Log 1824
Brownie Sundae Shortcakes 1812
Bunny Sundaes 1815
Buttermilk-Lime Sherbet 1809
Calypso Sundaes 1815
Cantaloupe Alaska 1825
Celebration Fruit Sherbet 1811
Cherry-Crème Parfaits 1819
Cherry Fudge Sundaes 1811
Chocolate Ice Cream Supreme 1802
Chocolate Mint Parfaits 1818
Chocolate Mint Sundaes 1811
Chocolate Skyscrapers 1812
Choffee Alaska 1825
Christmas Eggnog Sundae Ring 1815
Christmas Ice Cream Log 1822
Coconut Cream Ring 1822
Coffee-Almond Sparkle Sundaes 1814
Coffee Meringue Glacé 1826
Cranberry Ice 1809
Cranberry Tortoni 1808
Double Fudge Sundaes 1811
Double Orange Coupe 1810

1920

Double Strawberry Sundaes 1816
Dublin Ice Cream Bombe 1821
Frosty Fruit Cream 1804
Frozen Eggnog Cheese Squares 1808
Frozen Grape-Cream Cups 1806
Frozen Strawberry Crown 1822
Frozen Strawberry Mallo 1804
Frozen Strawberry Soufflé 1804
Grape Ice 1809
Hazelnut Cream Bombe 1819
Holiday Ice Cream 1810
Honey-Butter Sundaes 1815
Hot Fudge Sundaes 1811
Ice-Cream Fluff 1810
"Instant" Peach-Orange Sherbet 1809
Italian Ice 1809
Jubilee Sunday Stacks 1816
Kona Sundaes 1814
Lace-Wafer Sundaes 1812
Lemon Snow Sherbet 1809
Maple Butter-Nut Charlotte 1805
Meringue Fantastique 1826
Mexican Cream Torte 1822
Milk-Chocolate Ice Cream 1802
Milk-Chocolate Mousse 1803
Mocha Fudge Sundaes 1811
Old-Fashioned Vanilla Ice Cream 1802
Orange Blossom Ice Cream 1806
Paradise Parfaits 1818
Parfait Amandes 1808
Peach Fiesta Splits 1817
Peachy Parfaits 1819
Pear Splits 1817
Peppermint Fudge Sundaes 1812
Peppermint Snowballs 1818
Pineapple Sherbet in Orange Cups 1808
Pink and White Angel Sundaes 1817
Quick Butterscotch Sundaes 1814
Rainbow Ice Cream Cake 1823
Rainbow Party Pie 1826
Raspberry Alaskas 1824
Raspberry Mousse 1805
Regal Rio Sundaes 1811
Ribbon Ice Cream Cake 1823
Royal Baked Alaska 1824
Sinker Sundaes 1814
Spumoni 1810
Strawberry-Pink Mousse 1804
Strawberry Sundae Cake 1817
Strawberry Sundae Pizza 1816
Sunshine Dessert Bowl 1824
Triple Cream Bombe 1820
Tutti-Frutti Parfaits 1819
Walnut Bombe Alaska 1820
Watermelon Ice 1810

Dessert Sauces and Toppings:
Burnt-Sugar Sauce 1806
Butterscotch Sauce 1828
Butterscotch Sparkle Sauce 1829
Caramel Sundae Sauce 1812
Chocolate-Nut Sauce 1828

Chocolate Sundae Sauce 1828
Chocolate Truffle Sauce 1827
Chocolate Velvet Sauce 1827
Creamy Rum Sauce 1829
Currant Sparkle Sauce 1830
Easy Mocha Sauce 1828
Fluffy Vanilla Sauce 1829
Fluffy Wine Sauce 1829
Golden Butterscotch Sauce 1826
Golden Fruit Sauce 1830
Hot Fudge Sauce 1827
Java Sauce 1828
Jiffy Fudge Sauce 1827
Lemon Sparkle Sauce 1826
Maple Fluff Sauce 1830
Marshmallow Sauce 1829
Mint Fudge Sauce 1827
Mocha Sauce 1827
Orange Crowns 1835
Pink Peppermint Sauce 1830
Praline Sauce 1828
Raspberry Sauce 1825
Rio Chocolate Sauce 1811
Sparkle Ice Cream Sauce 1829
Strawberry Topping 1817
Toffee-Walnut Sauce 1829

Candies:
Candied Orange Slices 1804
Chocolate Fans 1812

Cookies:
Lace Wafers 1814

Beverages:
Apricot Frost 1835
Basic Chocolate Soda 1830
Black Cherry Bounce 1832
Candy-Stick Float 1833
Choco-Banana Flip 1834
Chocolate-Cherry Cooler 1833
Chocolate Milk Shake 1832
Chocolate Mint Soda 1831
Chocolate-Orange Fizz 1832
Chocolate-Peppermint Shake 1833
Citrus Soda 1832
Coffee-Cola Soda 1831
Coffee Ice Cream Soda 1831
Double Chocolate Soda 1830
Double Strawberry Dream 1834
Ginger-Orange Ice Cream Soda 1832
Maple-Pecan Milk Shake 1832
Mocha Ice Cream Soda 1831
Orange Ice Cream Soda 1831
Orange-Pineapple Whirl 1833
Orange-Vanilla Freeze 1835
Peach Dream 1835
Peach Frosty 1835
Peach Ice Cream Soda 1831
Peanut Whizz 1835
Raspberry Ice Cream Soda 1831
Rio Cream 1834
Strawberry Ice Cream Soda 1831
Strawberry Smoothie 1834
Sunburst Soda 1832
Super Mocha Milk Shake 1834
Tutti-Frutti Blush 1834
Vanilla Milk Shake 1832
Vermont Soda 1832